SHAME ON THE MOON

Unleashing the Past
A Memoir

Paul Dean Jackson

*To Rev. Carol
Who understands + Uses
The Force
with Aloha*

Tall Paul

X-MAS 2015

PAUL DEAN JACKSON

Shame on the Moon: Unleashing the Past, A Memoir
Copyright @ 2015 by Paul Dean Jackson

Paul Dean Jackson
www.pauldeanjackson.com

ISBN: 978-1-62249-300-5
Library of Congress Control Number: 2015944991

Editor: Jeannine Mallory
Interior Book & Jacket Design:
Every attempt has been made to source properly all quotes.

Printed in United States of America
For additional copies, visit:
www.pauldeanjackson.com

Published by The Educational Publisher Inc.
Biblio Publishing
BiblioPublishing.com

Disclaimer

Although this memoir is a true story, some people's names have been changed to protect their privacy. In all other senses, this book is an honest look from my own perspective about my life.

For my daughters, Katelyn and Kyra Skye.

CONTENTS

~v~

PROLOGUE

I was born at a unique intersection in history; there were those who knew and lived the life of segregation, and those who did not.

CHAPTER 1

STRAIGHT OUTTA COMPTON

It was a warm summer morning in Southern California. I was awakened at dawn by the familiar clatter of milk bottles outside our house. Wiping dried crust from the corners of my eyes, I jumped out of bed and raced to the window just in time to see the Carnation milkman rushing off with our empty milk bottles. Wasting no time, he trotted across the street, climbed into his shiny red and white truck, which was always left idling, and sped away. He left behind two icy-cold, half-gallon bottles of fresh whole milk, which he gently placed on our brightly painted red concrete porch.

I watched contently as he drove past the neighborhood's bungalow-style homes and conducted the early-morning ritual a few houses away. Every front lawn was lush, green, and neatly manicured. Hibiscus and bird of paradise flowers were in full bloom. As the sound of the milk truck faded, I quietly unlocked the front door, doing my best not to wake my family. I turned the squeaky doorknob slowly, trying not to make a sound, then gave the front door a gentle push. As the door cracked, the sound of songbirds flooded the room, and warm morning air pushed inside. Peering out, I reached down to pick up the milk a couple of feet from the doorway. I watched streams of water roll down the frosty sides of the bottles. I gripped them as tightly as I could with my tiny hands, carefully brought them inside, and tiptoed to the kitchen a few feet away.

Still being as quiet as possible, I climbed onto the kitchen counter, opened the cupboard, and strained to reach a box of cereal just out of my grasp.

On this special morning, I would not have the usual lumpy oatmeal served by my mother, whose talent in the kitchen was limited to canned vegetables and liver and onions. Nor would I be enjoying the All-American family favorite, Corn Flakes, which stayed crunchy in milk for approximately fifty-nine seconds before turning to the consistency of snot.

This morning was like no other. I beckoned the cereal closer to me by stretching my index finger around the bottom edge of the box. Finally, I pulled an unopened box of Kellogg's Sugar Pops into view. The night before, while on the family's "big shopping trip," as we referred to our trip to the market, I'd coaxed my mother into buying them.

Once a month, after the bills were paid (I always begged for the privilege of licking the stamps and envelopes, which had a pleasant minty flavor), my mother went to Rosecrans Plaza, around the corner from our house, to Safeway for groceries. Since we had to make do with whatever food was in the house until she got her paycheck (my mother was a librarian), we called it the "big shopping trip" because when we got to the checkout line, our shopping basket was always full. My sisters and I loved to tag along because we could usually talk our mother into buying each of us one of our favorite food items.

I laid the groundwork weeks in advance by incessantly singing the theme to a television commercial implanted in my five-year-old brain. "Oh, the Pops are sweeter, and the taste is new. They're shot with sugar through and through. Sugar Pops are *tops!*"

Once inside Safeway, I raised the volume as we neared the cereal aisle. Eventually, my mother got the "hint," and to my great surprise, dropped the Pops into our shopping cart seconds before my singing turned to a full-blown convulsion of the begging and pleading song and dance performed by most five-year-olds.

Now, with my sisters still asleep, I was free to gorge myself with the wonderful morsels of toasted sugarcoated corn. This morning, I dispensed with my usual cereal bowl, and with no regard for anyone else, filled a large salad bowl to the rim. Removing the top from the freshly delivered milk proved to be more of an undertaking, but with a great deal of effort, I managed. My hands shook and my skinny arms were unsteady as I filled the bowl until the cereal floated to the top and cascaded onto the table. Scrambling for the overflowing morsels like a miner who had just discovered a gold nugget in the river, I shoved them into my mouth, savoring the sugary flavor. Uninterrupted, I devoured the entire bowl, and then slowly drank the sugar-flavored milk, savoring every drop as a connoisseur might sip a vintage wine. As the skin began to tighten around my slender tummy, I displayed a happy Buddha belly. "What a feast," I thought. Little did I realize that it might be my last.

We lived in Compton, a small suburb roughly ten miles south of downtown Los Angeles. Compton was known as "The Hub City" because of its location between the L.A. Civic Center, the City of Long Beach, and L.A. Harbor.

In 1960, Compton was booming. Tract homes and new businesses replaced fertile farmlands as the area began to take on a new face...a black face. Whites were leaving Compton in droves, bound for points further south toward an imaginary line where minorities were not welcome—the white haven known as Orange County. Our neighbors and fellow church members at Saint Timothy Episcopal in Compton were creating a new phenomenon, which coincided with the arrival of the church's newest Negro congregants. It was a mass exodus, soon to be termed "white flight."

> The city once known for its prize-winning produce and livestock fast became a haven for black middle-class homeowners by the 1960s. The election of the first black mayor of a major California municipality in 1969 brought Compton unwanted scrutiny from a sensation hungry media all too willing to work from stereotypes. Stigmatized as a high-crime combat zone in the 1970s and 1980s, homegrown gangster-rap artists solidified the myth of Compton as the home of the deprived and depraved.

> — From *Images of America: Compton*
> by Robert Lee Johnson

I am here to testify that "back in the day," Compton was a wonderful place to live. Downtown was neat, clean, and thriving. It was the dawn of the space age. We heard the startling sound of progress in the jarring double bang of a sonic boom followed by the rattle of window glass and frayed nerves. X-Planes regularly pushed the envelope of the outer limits of earth, reaching hypersonic speeds over Southern California's Mojave Desert. Cars with wings or elaborate tailfins cruised Compton Boulevard. Downtown bustled with activity as shoppers pressed shoulder to shoulder on the sidewalk with bags from J.J. Newberry, J.C. Penney, and other department stores that lined the street. Family trips to downtown Compton (the L.A. Civic Center was simply know as Downtown) usually meant a visit to Woolworth's, where we nestled up to the lunch counter and enjoyed a treat from the soda fountain. In those days, a dollar really meant something. It was ten cents for a king-size

Coca-Cola, twenty-five cents for ice cream sundaes, and my favorite banana splits were just thirty-nine cents.

Back then, commuter rail was the preferred mode of transportation. Trains known as the Red Line connected Compton to downtown L.A. and points between.

I often rode with my dad to the train station to drop off my mother, whose library branch was in Los Angeles. I watched her board the Red Car. Pacific Electric, a privately-owned mass transit system, consisted of streetcars, light rail, and buses. My mother always took a window seat, then turned and gazed upon me with concern as the train, which was usually comprised of just two cars, slowly pulled away from the station.

When we returned home, my father would soon be off to his job. He was a physiotherapist at Las Campanas Hospital in Compton. The hospital and ancillary buildings spanned several acres. Few were aware of the secret hidden behind the huge white walls that all but enclosed the entire facility. Behind those walls, secluded from prying eyes, was a sanitarium. It was the place where some of Hollywood's greatest stars went to dry out. Screen legend Judy Garland, who was known for her recurrent mental breakdowns, was a frequent visitor.

While our parents were at work, we were left in the care of my older sister, Elizabeth. It wasn't uncommon back then for parents to leave children home alone. We were latchkey kids, meaning you had a shoestring with a house key tied around your neck, and you let yourself into the house after school. I thought it was an honor to wear the house key. I hadn't been bestowed with the privilege, so I wore a different key, a skate key.

PAUL DEAN JACKSON

Looking back, it seems like virtually every kid in our neighborhood owned roller skates. Not so much because we wanted them, but because most of our parents couldn't afford to buy us bicycles.

Our skates were steel-wheeled monstrosities that were assembled with a hex key. The coarse wheels required frequent oiling to keep them spinning freely. The key was used to adjust the length and fit of the skate. You just squeezed your sneakers between what looked like two bullhorns in the front of the skate, then pushed or pulled it to fit the length of your foot. Roller skates may have coined the phrase "one size fits all," but not very well. Many a child took a tumble because your foot could easily pop out of the toe clips. With a little skill and a lot of luck, you could bunny-hop your way to a grassy landing on someone's front lawn, where you could grab your skate key, squeeze the toe clips, re-fasten them tightly, and be on your way. But mostly, the result was a Band-Aid over skinned knees.

When I wasn't on my roller skates, I was in our backyard playing on an old swing set. The swings were broken, and the chains that once held them were rusted and left to dangle. My favorite activity was to climb atop the crossbar and survey the goings on in the neighbors' backyards. Quietly perched there, I was able to look over a tall wooden fence and spy on the family next door.

Mrs. Sauers was a grumpy woman whom I always heard yelling at the top of her lungs at her children. I couldn't pronounce her name and called her Mrs. Sour. Oddly enough, no one ever corrected me. If her kids misbehaved (which was almost daily), she'd emerge from the house with a thick leather belt in one hand, and then herd them inside while whipping their butts along the way. I witnessed many a spanking from my perch.

Our backyard was not big. Ivy covered a brick wall in the back. There was a small, detached garage on the side. Our play area was next to the garage, completely secluded behind the house on both sides by the fence.

As these were tract homes, the Sauers pretty much had the same layout in their yard, but they'd converted their garage into a family room.

On this day, the day of my Sugar Pops feast, "Mrs. Sour" happened to be in her backyard checking on a litter of newborn kittens the family cat had hidden behind their family room. I had no wish to talk to her, so before she could spot me, I grabbed the dangling chain to swing down to the ground and out of her sight. I had performed this vanishing act dozens of times before.

When I began my descent, my foot slipped off the cross bar, causing me to lose my grip on the chain, which popped high into the air, and then flipped over my head, forming a perfect noose. Suddenly, I found myself dangling precariously by my neck. My feet didn't reach the ground, and the rusty chain bit into my skin.

I clearly remember thinking, "How embarrassing. Now Mrs. Sour is gonna see me." I wiggled to regain my footing on the cross bar, which caused the chain to form a tighter noose. The bar was too high for me to gain a foothold. I tried to reach the teeter-totter on the edge of the swing set, in hopes of climbing up it to the cross bars, but it was just out of my reach.

Being only five years old, I had no idea of the dire predicament I was in. I had no thought of what appeared to be my impending death. As the chain cut into my neck, I continued calmly to look around the yard to see what other avenues of escape might be available to me. Dangling there, but now beginning to choke, I realized there were none.

I have no idea why Mrs. Sour decided to look over the fence into our backyard at that moment. Perhaps it was the rattle of the chain, or maybe she heard the faint sound of my quiet struggle. Perhaps it was intuition.

I remember the look of sheer panic on her face as she watched me dangling there, choking to death. Apparently, she knew there was no way in the world she could scale the fence, so she wallowed out of sight. With my legs now twitching like a doomed man over the hangman's trap door, my breathing became labored. I was in peril. At that moment, the gate burst open. Mrs. Sour rounded the corner, rushed over, and gently lifted me up and out of my noose of death. My neck was scratched and bleeding from the rusty chain. Even as I was about to take what would have been my last breath…I knew I would not die.

I believe I was spared that day and put on this earth for a reason, a reason the universe would reveal to me later in life.

CHAPTER 2

FAMILY

By today's standards, I grew up in an abusive household. In the 1960s, corporeal punishment was not the exception; it was the rule. "Spare the rod, spoil the child," went the saying, and so went my youth.

Television shaped my childhood. By watching TV, I learned the definition of feminine beauty, Lady Clairol; and blondes had more fun. I knew unequivocally that a man who used a little dab of Brylcreem could have any woman he desired. Television bent my view of the world, and at five years old, I soaked it all in as gospel.

Blacks were dumb; whites were smart. White was right. If you're black, get back. Indians were bloodthirsty savages. Mexicans were banditos. Asians were either "Chinamen" or "Dirty Japs."

Sitting on the living room couch in front of our black-and-white RCA Victor TV, my mind was an open book. Thankfully, my manual to American society allowed me to observe a "normal" family's life. I took solace from *Father Knows Best* and sought refuge with the Cleavers. Never once did I see Beaver get a spanking.

If I wanted to explore the wilderness, I could take an adventure with Timmy and Lassie. The pair communicated famously during their TV run, and I got it. I understood

"Dog," really. Long before the term "dog whisperer" existed, I was talking to dogs, cats, and, yes, even birds.

At the time, the pet of choice for boys in Compton was not dogs or cats, but pigeons. If you listened closely, you could hear the gentle cooing of the birds from backyard pigeon coops. My neighbor, Edward Hearld, owned more than a dozen, and from the moment I set my eyes on them, I wanted a bird.

As it happened, my grandmother was visiting us. My Grandma Dean was a big woman of Bohemian descent, who stood tall and straight. She was a woman of means who spoiled the child and spared the rod as only a grandmother could.

She took me to the pet store and allowed me to pick out any pigeons I wanted. It should not be at all surprising (because of my affinity to white families on TV) that I chose white birds. I chose a male, whom I named King, and his mate, Queen.

When I got them home, Edward took one look and scowled. "A couple of commies," he said. "Commies" was the term used for domestic pigeons, with no redeeming pedigree characteristics (they were *common*).

At six years old, I knew nothing of the wide variety of breeds, from rollers to homing racers. King and Queen lived in a coop behind the house. I spent many days out there. King was the first of many animals I bonded with over the years. Any time I was outside, he flew to me and landed on my shoulder. It was fine with me, but not so much for my mother, who had to do the laundry.

We were the closest of friends. This bird actually followed me around the neighborhood. I'd spy him on a power line watching over me while I played with friends. "Go home, King," I would demand. And he usually did.

It wasn't long before King and Queen had squabs. My mother joked about eating them, telling me how tasty squab was. She never got a taste, as I either traded or sold them. By the time I was nine, I owned twenty-one pigeons. Fan Tails, Muffs, homing racers, and even a coveted Birmingham roller, which wandered into the trap door of my coop when he was a squab. My collection of exotic birds was worth hundreds of dollars. But I didn't love money; I loved King, who remained my favorite. When Grandma Dean came to visit, I could tell watching King and me together brought her joy.

CHAPTER 3

FROM RAGS TO RICHES

In the '60s, conversations about race were a prerequisite within the African-American community. If it were a college course, it would have been called "Being Colored 101," with a special emphasis on the amount of Caucasian or Indian blood you carried, especially if it showed in the texture of your hair or the color of your skin.

My mother told me that in order to join a black sorority when she was in college, you had to pass the paper bag test. The test was simple; if your skin was lighter than a paper bag, you could pledge. If it was darker, you could not. I grew up in a system that taught young children that the more white blood you possessed, the more desirable you were. That was normal to us. Being black was not beautiful; it was a scourge.

Broken into a mathematical formula, my ethnicity was just acceptable to the black bourgeoisie. I am 69 percent black, 19 percent white, and 12 percent Native American. Thankfully, I have never thought of myself as anything other than black because I once believed that being multicultural in a world of black and white must have been a living hell.

When I mentioned my grandmother was a woman of means, it may have been a gross understatement. Her father pioneered a section of South Florida known as Coconut Grove. He and his wife lived the quintessential American success story, amassing enormous wealth through backbreaking labor. History remembers them as the most important family in the evolution of the black Bahamian Grove in South Florida, but our family version is a bit more intriguing.

Ebenezer Woodberry Franklin Stirrup was the illegitimate son of a slave. But not just any slave. His mother was a Bahamian servant, and her employer (I say "employer" because slavery ended five years before his birth) was a wealthy white landowner on Harbour Island in the Bahamas.

According to family lore, Ebenezer's white father was proud of his son, not only accepting him as blood, but also handing over the keys to the kingdom by offering his progeny a place by his side.

"He was his own man," recalled my grandmother. "He rejected slavery and his father," she said, with a tone both proud and determined.

At the tender age of fifteen, Ebenezer left his island home in a tiny boat and set sail for the mainland to live with his uncle and seek his fortune in America.

"He was deeply in love and promised his childhood sweetheart he would return for her one day," recalls my mother.

Young Stirrup's skiff landed in the Florida Keys, where, under the tutelage of his uncle, a carpenter, he learned the skills of woodworking and construction. They were skills that would prove useful in the years to come. Driven by the power of love, he remained in Key West for nearly a decade, until he saved enough money to return to the Bahamas for his childhood sweetheart, Charlotte Sawyer, whom he married.

With his new bride in tow, Stirrup returned to the U.S. and moved north to Perrine, a small community between Miami and Homestead. There, he found opportunity knocking. Hearty newcomers were flocking to the region located along Biscayne Bay by the lure of land and opportunity.

Now a skilled carpenter, Ebenezer went to work for William Cutler, a medical doctor from Massachusetts. Dr. Cutler first visited the area in the 1870s and fell in love with the region. He returned years later and purchased a 600-acre tract of land for $1.25 per acre. With my great-grandfather's help, Cutler set out to establish a fruit and vegetable plantation. In lieu of cash, Cutler often paid my great-grandfather in land, the source of what would become a vast accumulation of valuable real estate.

The way my grandmother tells it, Ebenezer and "Old Man Cutler," as she called him, were fast friends. My grandmother was the first of ten children (six of whom survived into adulthood). After toiling all day on Old Man Cutler's estate, Ebenezer hiked more than four miles through the thicket and mangroves to Coconut Grove, the spot he chose to build his home. There was little time for rest as Stirrup burned the midnight oil, working through the night until he was able to complete construction on a home of his own.

My great-grandfather's good fortune continued. He befriended, and traded with, Seminole Indians. After enduring three wars with the United States, they called themselves the "Unconquered People." The man my grandfather traded with was likely one of just 200 to 300 Indians who were able to elude capture and forced relocation by the U.S. Army. My mother loved to tell the story of a Seminole who came to visit Grandpa Stirrup at his homestead in Coconut Grove.

"Grandmother Dean was just a little girl. She took one look at the approaching brave and screamed bloody murder," my mother said, laughing. "Well, he was just wearing a loincloth. Grandpa rushed outside and saw the man and was mad as hell," she said, still laughing. My mother explained the Indian was one of my grandfather's friends, and he was deeply embarrassed by his daughter's fearful behavior. "Go inside you silly girl," he demanded.

In my grandmother's defense, aside from horror stories from whites about past Indian wars, little was seen of the Florida Seminole until they began to venture out and trade in the late nineteenth century.

Stirrup continued his life of labors with Charlotte Jane by his side. Together, they amassed a small empire, purchasing land and constructing more than 100 homes. Despite his lack of a formal education, Stirrup became a formidable businessman and owned a grocery store, bicycle repair shop, tailor shop, meat market, private horse and buggy transportation, two cemeteries, and a dry goods store. Through his years of hard work and business acumen, Stirrup eventually became Florida's first black millionaire, owning a variety of properties in Coconut Grove, Cutler, and Overtown.

Since my grandmother was the oldest family member, it fell upon her to oversee the vast empire when her father died. Up until that time, she was the dean of an all-girls' school in Miami. She took the job after the death of her husband, a Florida businessman by the name of Fredrick Dean.

"They called her Dean Dean," my mother joyfully recalls.

In a 1976 interview, my grandmother recalled, "Father believed in every family having a house, a yard, and a garden, so you would feel like you had a home. He felt that people became better citizens when they owned their own homes."

With little business experience, she was ill prepared to be the overseer of this vast estate. She sold many of her family's properties in order to pay taxes.

The part of my family's story that intrigues me is the fact that Old Man Cutler not only paid my great-grandfather in cash, but also in land. And though we can't confirm it, it is believed Ebenezer Woodberry Franklin Stirrup owned upwards of 100 acres of land on Cutler's estate.

My grandmother claims she was swindled out of that land by folks she referred to as "unscrupulous Jewish lawyers."

Poring over historic text in an attempt to sort out the truth, I learned that Dr. Cutler tried, unsuccessfully, to convince many of his friends to settle in the area. Only one, William Fuzzard, took him up on the offer. History credits Fuzzard as being the area's founding father. He later named the area "Cutler" to honor his friend.

Fuzzard eventually moved to North Miami, along with fifty or so other residents, when the railroad bypassed the area.

For the next fifty years, Cutler Ridge mostly belonged to deer, panthers, waterfowl, and snakes. And somewhere in the middle of those mangroves, open glades, and creeping vines…was Great-Grandpa's land.

In the early '50s, David Bloomberg began developing the land on Cutler Ridge. The first housing development went up in 1954; six years later, a mall opened. The timeframe seems to jibe precisely with Grandma's story.

Taking today's property values into account, that undocumented 100 acres of prime real estate on the Intercoastal could be valued in the billions, as it is now some of the most expensive real estate on the planet.

The Stirrup family still owns a number of properties in Coconut Grove and surrounding areas under the Stirrup Properties brand, which remains family owned and operated.

My mother's life story has never been clear, at least to me. It was as if she suffered from selective amnesia. I concluded something dark must have happened to her in Florida. She was named Charlotte, after her grandmother. She claims to have had a happy life surrounded by people who loved her. But the moment she graduated from college, she turned her back on her family's wealth and headed west, never to return.

She knows little of her father. "He was a businessman from Miami who died when I was very young." Getting information about Frederick Dean from my mother was like extracting teeth without anesthesia. I eventually learned that he was a widower who had two daughters before he married my grandmother and they became a blended family. I found it odd that she did not care to know who this man was. When I inquired, she would become troubled, saying, "I didn't know my father. He died when we were very young, but we had a happy life. We just didn't think about him."

After her husband passed, Grandma Dean moved in with Grandpa (EWF Stirrup, as our family lovingly referred to him), leaving her stepdaughters to live with her husband's relatives. The half-sisters never spoke or interacted as a family again.

"Grandpa" and his wife Charlotte helped raised my mother and her little sister Dazelle. It is strange not to know what to call Charlotte Jane. I've never had to articulate the word "Great-Grandmother," as both of my great-grandmothers passed away long before I could speak.

Aunt Dazelle married a New York "city slicker" named George Simpson. My great-grandfather, who did not have a high school diploma, made sure all his children received a higher education. Stirrup financed the couple's college educations, and they went on to become physicians. Aunt Dazelle became the first black pediatrician in the state. And Uncle George went on to become the first black surgeon in Florida. They eventually built and operated a hospital together to fill the gap in the underserved needs of South Florida's black residents.

My mother, meanwhile, attended Fisk University and obtained a Master's degree in library science. She says she left Florida to escape racism. But in 1940, there were few safe havens. Fresh out of college, she moved west to Los Angeles, where she married. My mother admits she knew very little about my father before they were married. They met at a sorority dance, and my mother said she really wasn't that interested in him. She had another suitor at the dance, but my father was persistent, and as for the other gent, apparently not so.

My father, Paul Moore Jackson, was a dashing young physical therapist. But, as my mother would learn, he had a hidden past. My dad hated being black, and he constantly reminded us he was part Indian. Unlike my mother, he spun amazing tales of his family. The story of his grandfather never changed and always absorbed me.

Josiah Jackson, according to my father, was an Oregon lumberjack. Not any lumberjack, but very possibly the predecessor to the great Paul Bunyan. Honestly, who's to say? Paul Bunyan's exploits evolved from the tall tales of North American loggers. Could it be possible that the legend of Paul Bunyan evolved from the exploits of my great-grandfather?

According to my dad, his grandfather was 6'10." He was a giant. "He could carry a barrel in one arm and a grown man in the other," explained my father.

Hmm, a giant lumberjack with superhuman strength in the woods of Oregon. Sure sounds like Paul Bunyan to me. In none of his stories, however, did my father mention a blue ox named Babe.

The story fascinated me so much that I traveled to Oregon and spent a week in the heat of summer poring over archives at the natural history museum in Portland. I combed through historical text, hoping to find a story about the giant in the woods. Unfortunately, I could not find a single word about this mysterious black giant.

I did learn that it was a crime to be black in Oregon. Blacks and mulattos were not permitted to live in the state during the time that my great-grandfather would have lived here. In fact, there were laws on the books that free black people would be subject to flogging if found in the territory.

I can only assume my great-grandfather stayed as far away from whites and civilization as possible. Exactly how a black man got to Oregon in the time of slavery was a mystery. Was he a runaway slave? Where was he from?

Then I began to have a recurring dream. Deep in REM sleep, I saw a tall, bearded black man wearing buckskin clothing running across the early-American landscape. Native Americans pursued him, but they couldn't catch him. Tribe after tribe tried, but always failed. He was simply too strong, too fast, and too determined in his stride as he made his way Northwest. These pursuits were agonizing. In my dreams, he ran for days on end until his pursuers, who were also on foot, finally realized he was impossible prey. My dream of his odyssey played out countless times, and always ended the same. Bewildered braves gave up the chase, then gave him their version of "the finger" before heading back to their villages.

One night, my dream changed. I'd never paid attention to the surroundings, which were always a vague, dry, western landscape, with barrel cactus amidst the rugged terrain. This night, the pursuit took place in a forest. At full gait, he bounded over downed trees and splashed through a small stream until he reached a clearing. Directly ahead were a sheer rock face and waterfall. Hearing the distant footsteps of the pursuers, he pressed on until he reached an impassable river.

An Indian woman with a papoose strapped to her back stood on the riverbank. He stopped and gazed at her. By then, braves had reached the riverbank. They approached cautiously, then froze. They seemed mesmerized by his stature, and it was clear that none had ever seen a black man.

In this dream, I realized Jackson had an axe in his hand. The war party slowly fanned out and surrounded him. Hopelessly outnumbered, he gripped his axe tightly. Suddenly, the sound of cracking twigs broke the silence. The Indian woman he had seen earlier came out of hiding from behind a fallen tree. He looked at her contently, and then walked slowly toward the war party. It was the only time he ever spoke in my dreams. It was a single word.

"No."

He looked at the child strapped to the woman's back, and then, ever so gently, tossed his axe aside.

The braves studied him closely; all stood in silence. I sensed they were in awe of his height, his strength, and now, his humanity. One of the braves gave him a knowing nod, and then they turned, one by one, and left him in peace.

Since I have been robbed of my history, I like to believe the story in my dream is true. Perhaps it's a "knowing," a vision of the past. Against all odds, my great-grandfather escaped slavery and made his way across the United States until he arrived at the banks of the Columbia River in Oregon and could run no further.

Though my great-grandfather was an enigma, I easily located my grandfather in the historical archives. Lewis Edward Jackson attended the Hill Military School in Portland, Oregon. He left the Pacific Northwest at some point in his young life and moved to the San Francisco Bay area, where he met his wife-to-be, a Mohawk half-breed (as society referred to biracial Native Americans at the time) named Elizabeth. Ironically, her last name was also Jackson.

"Scotch Irish. He was a Scotch Irish trader," my dad would say, referring to his white grandfather. It mattered not that he'd married outside his race. When his daughter fell in love with a black man, he became enraged. My father says that he did everything in his power to keep the young lovers apart. When that failed, he sent his daughter east to live with relatives. But their love for one another was strong, so she saved her money and returned west. The Jacksons married and began a family.

Lewis Jackson was a brilliant man. He found work as a chemist in the wine industry, a job that required constant travel. The Jacksons settled in Oakland, where they had three children: Eloise, her younger sister, Margaret, and my father.

Anguish filled my father's face when he spoke of Margaret. His features hardened as tears began to fill his eyes. "She was kicked in the head by a mule and died."

It was the first time I saw my father cry.

My dad was a tall, thin, athletic man who stood 6'5". His complexion was "red-boned," showing his mixed heritage. The native Californian grew up with a love of nature. He was a boxing enthusiast, tennis player, and an impressive distance runner, specializing in the 3,200-meter event in track.

But this native son had a dark side. He failed to inform my mother he had a history. My mother was his third wife. To compound matters, soon after they were married, he became abusive.

Despite his hang-ups (and he had many), my father was a proud man. He did not allow my mother to accept any money from her family. His directive fell on deaf ears when it came to her little sister Dazelle. Did I mention that Dazelle was a force?

"One day she called me," my mother recalled with delight. "She said, 'Go pick up your new car.'"

"What?" replied my mother.

Aunt Dazelle said, "Go pick up your new car at Bill Barnett Chevrolet in Compton." She had paid cash for our family's first new vehicle because she did not want her big sister to use public transportation.

Aside from that extravagant surprise, and the story my beloved mother enjoyed telling, we lived quite a different existence from our rich relatives in Florida. My cousins had a live-in maid, who cooked, cleaned, and served as their surrogate mother. They never had to lift a finger, as far as sharing in household chores.

My family, on the other hand, lived a very different life. I had no idea my mother came from money. While our first cousins grew up with the proverbial "silver spoon," I was happy with our "stainless-steel" lifestyle in Compton.

My parents had four children, but not by my mother's design. Their firstborn was Elizabeth, named after my father's mother. Soon after, Margaret arrived. Two girls were enough for my mother. She was done having babies, and went to the family doctor for an IUD. Unfortunately, the technology of the day was new, and so along came my sister Paula.

Until Paula, there'd been no indication that my parents were both part white. Paula emerged from the womb a white baby. My father was elated because she looked like his mother. And so, for a time, they were a happy family of three.

My mother had no qualms in telling me about her second IUD failure. "I was mad as hell at the doctor," she told me later in her life. Nothing like knowing you weren't a wanted child. Thank God I was a boy. Otherwise, I might've been flushed. My father, on the other hand, was pleased to have a son.

All families have problems. So I won't trouble you with the gory specifics within mine. I will say that as the years passed, my father became physically abusive, lashing out at his oldest child, Elizabeth. I was too young to know why he beat her. Margaret always went to her rescue, only to be attacked herself. This pattern went on for years. Paula and I were somewhat shielded because she looked like his mother, and I learned to lie low and stay out of sight.

My mother says she stayed with my father for our sake, believing it was the right thing to do. But as time went on, Elizabeth became more defiant. She seemed to be deliberately trying to pull my father's strings, knowing the results would be more beatings. My mother looked on helplessly, never once intervening to stop him.

My parents stayed together almost seventeen years. Sadly, by the time their divorce was final, the cycle of abuse had evolved. Elizabeth became the abuser. Because of her emotional pain, she deliberately set out to destroy Paula's and my sense of self-worth through the same verbal and physical abuse she received.

Our cries for help fell on deaf ears. Now a single mother and the family's sole breadwinner, my mother immersed herself in her career. She rose to the top of her profession, ultimately turning down the number two position in the Los Angeles Public Library System. She chose instead to remain head of the southern region. I think it had something to do with her office in San Pedro. The San Pedro branch was a new facility, the crown jewel of the L.A. Library system.

Ultimately, my mother's absence from family life elevated Elizabeth to the position of primary caregiver, and her cruelty escalated. She seemed to hate Paula more with each passing day. It took years of psychological counseling before Paula and I finally realized that Elizabeth despised that my father could not hide the fact that Paula was his favorite. Very simply put, my dad loved Paula more because her skin was white.

Paula began to have trouble on two fronts. First, there was Elizabeth's constant verbal and physical abuse. And then, there were the girls in our neighborhood who didn't like her because she was "high yellow," which was the term for light-skinned blacks.

My mother allowed Elizabeth's abusive behavior because of the immense sense of guilt she felt from never stopping my father's abuse.

The rift between my oldest sister and me grew far beyond childhood and took an unexpected twist when Elizabeth did the unfathomable. It was something so deceitful and sinister that my life changed forever. More about that later.

"To understand is to forgive, even oneself."

— Alexander Chase

Two stories about my father empowered me to forgive his past transgressions.

"We knew our grandfather," he told me. "When he saw us walking down the street with our mother, he crossed to the other side." The bitter old man never met his grandchildren, nor did he ever speak to his daughter again. It was clear to me that my father loved his mother and big sister more than anything in the world.

"Every day after school, we waited for our mother at the public bus stop," he told me. "She sat in the front of the bus (she was thought to be white). We sat in the back. We had to pretend we didn't know her. We couldn't say hello or even acknowledge her as our mother until we got off the bus, were off the main street, and around the corner in our neighborhood."

I felt the anguish of his story deep in my soul. I tried to imagine what it was like to wait all day to see your mother, your everything, and then not be able to touch her, hug her, kiss her, or tell her you loved her.

Shame on the moon! It's enough to make anyone crazy.

That simple story of our racist society not only allowed me to forgive my father, but also gave me an insight into why he was the way he was.

I will always remember the warm summer days in Compton, standing on the corner waiting for my mother to walk home from the bus stop. "There she is! Mama," we would shout at the top of our lungs as we ran toward her as fast as our legs would carry us. Seeing her round the corner of our street is one of my happiest childhood memories. I would rush up to give her what I called a jawbreaker kiss, which was not perfect unless she said, "Ouch"…in a good way.

CHAPTER 4

CASA DOMINGUEZ

I don't recall getting any warning that we were going to leave our home in Compton for brand-new digs in Dominguez Hills, California. Our little bungalow-style home had three bedrooms, so we kids shared rooms. My father was old-fashioned and thought it wasn't prudent for a boy to share a room with a girl, and so I became the impetus for our new home.

At least that's what they told us. But in the summer of 1965, Compton changed forever. We lived just a block off Central Avenue, near the corner of Rosecrans. A little more than a mile up the street, two white police officers arrested two young black boys for drinking and driving. Their mother intervened, and a scuffle began. Finally, one of the officers cracked one of the boys over the head with his nightstick. The entire family was arrested. This event became the catalyst, the proverbial straw that broke the camel's back and began the Watts Riots.

Watts was a powder keg. The black people who lived there seemed angry. I could feel it every time I visited my mother at the Watts library. After years of economic isolation, the powder keg erupted and engulfed a fifty-mile area of South Central Los Angeles.

We had just moved into a brand-new home in Del Ammo Highlands, a development not far away. My father was apparently curious about what was going on in Watts, so he decided to see for himself. He took all of us kids along for the ride (without my mother's knowledge).

This time, the faces I saw on the street were not angry, but euphoric. I remember driving down Central Avenue with our windows down. Elizabeth had the brilliant idea that if someone shot at our car, the glass would not shatter in our faces.

We were in an active riot zone, but folks simply stared at us as we drove by. We were like spectators on a tour bus. Then it happened, the single thing about the Watts riots I will never forget. We'd stopped at a red light on Central Avenue when a National Guard convoy went screaming by. There were about seven vehicles. The last truck was a troop carrier towing a Jeep with a machine gun mounted on it. As it crossed the intersection, the troop carrier hit a bump, unlatching the Jeep, which sailed full speed into a service station across the street from us. It hit the gas pump with such force that sparks erupted from the impact. The convoy continued at breakneck speed, never noticing it had lost the Jeep. My father laughed hysterically (apparently at the stupidity) as did the crowd on the street next to us. It was all beyond my understanding. I was petrified, fearing the entire service station was about to explode and kill us and everyone else in the general vicinity.

Following the riots, leaving Compton and its charred ruins, traveling south down Wilmington Boulevard was like following the yellow brick road. Instead of poppies, thousands of flowering carnations lined the road. We lived near a flower farm. Brilliant yellow and bright red blanketed the hillside as far as the eye could see. The gusty Santa Ana winds fanned their fragrance. Grazing in the fields of flowers were grasshoppers; well, at least that's what I called them.

They went by many names: oil horses, donkey pumpers, dinosaurs; their official name is pump jack. The huge oil pumps were constantly in motion, pulling the area's black gold out of the ground.

The first time I laid eyes on a grasshopper, I fully intended to ride one at my first opportunity. Union Oil placed antennae on theirs and named them Uni-Hoppers. They became an instant hit with kids until someone died riding the wild beast. The cute antennae disappeared, and the grasshoppers were fenced in before I could get my chance.

I loved windy days, which ripped away L.A.'s eye-burning smog belt, and allowed picture postcard days to unfold.

As a child, I treasured those days. I remember driving from church in Compton toward the Port of Long Beach. On sunny, smog-free days, I could oversee my entire universe from a point atop the Dominguez Hills (which divide Los Angeles and Long Beach). Behind me stood the skyscrapers of Downtown Los Angeles, and behind them, a wall of mountains accentuated by a snowcapped Mount Baldy. Ahead, I could see the Rancho Palos Verdes Peninsula rising above the busy Los Angeles Harbor. On crystal-clear days like these, my eyes always followed the expanse of the Vincent Thomas Bridge from San Pedro to Long Beach, and then twenty-six miles out to sea for the most memorable sight of all. The awe-inspiring peaks of Santa Catalina Island rose majestically out of the Pacific.

The homes were beautiful and affordable. It took a brave young black woman (whose name I do not have) filing a discrimination suit against the builders to allow blacks to buy. We had the two-story, five-bedroom model. Back then, $32,500 went a long way. I immediately claimed an upstairs bedroom overlooking a huge vacant lot, which the contractors promised would be the site of a new elementary school.

We were on a bluff that overlooked farmland. Below our home, less than a mile away, stood the ominous ever-bellowing Shell Oil refinery. On the north-facing border rose a hundred-foot flare stack, which snarled and hissed day and night. On high production days, it illuminated the entire neighborhood, screaming an atrocious hiss while spitting flames high into the night sky. It was a terrifying spot that I intended to avoid.

Across what I called "The Big Street," Wilmington Boulevard, was a bluff that overlooked an open field. From the top, you could see the entire area known as Casa Dominguez, a community steeped in California history. The area was still home to every manner of critter: jackrabbits, garter snakes, horned toads, alligator lizards, possum, and even a crawdad pond.

As I explored the area on foot, I realized we had no neighbors. Rolling tumbleweeds seemed to put an explanation point on the fact that the entire neighborhood was deserted. We were the first family to move there. Or so I thought.

On the first morning in our new home, we gathered at the dining room table for our morning gruel. Sadly, my mother never perfected the art of making oatmeal. Suddenly, a head poked into view at the kitchen window. A Japanese boy gazed in, pressing his face hard against the glass to get a closer look inside. Soon another boy came into view, standing in the background. It was his older brother.

"It's okay, Paul. You can go outside if you want," said my mother.

And so I began the next phase of my childhood, with the Fujinami brothers as my friends.

The Fujinamis were the first residents of these new tract homes. Their family had owned and farmed the entire plot of land that was our neighborhood. Apparently, Mr. Fujinami exchanged the land for a new home. He still owned and worked a flower farm in Long Beach. At harvest, he always brought a bucket to our home for my mother.

It felt as if we lived in the country. The nearest development was nearly a mile away. The main street to the nearest store was a dirt road.

I knew a little about the country. My first vivid experience of the great outdoors began early one spring morning when my dad packed up the family for a weekend camping trip to Yosemite National Park.

A few days earlier and without notice (which was his style), my father arrived home in a slightly used Ford Country Squire station wagon. I'd never seen anything like it. A car made of wood? Whatever its make-up, this grand automobile belonged to us. It had three rows of seats, and the third row sported a rear-facing seat, which I claimed immediately.

We began our road trip in the middle of the night. As the early morning hours droned on, the road lulled my mother and sisters to sleep. As they snuggled and snored, I carefully worked my way from the third row to the front seat. Finally up front, I gazed over the dashboard to find we were on a mountainous stretch of highway with few guardrails and many jagged cliffs. While I considered my father an excellent driver, I wanted to ensure that he was fully alert and negotiating these hairpin curves at a prudent speed. It was the first time I stayed awake all night.

I marveled as the sunrise illuminated a forest kingdom filled with ancient redwoods so enormous that one served as a roadway tunnel.

We camped in canvas tents near Yosemite Creek. At the time, the babbling brook was so pristine (explained my father) you could drink from its banks. And so my dad and I walked to the water's edge, dropped as if ready to do push-ups, and dipped our heads into the fast-moving stream for a long, refreshing drink.

It was the first time in my young life I had ever truly tasted water. It was nothing like the hard water channeled through the desert to finally reach our tap in Compton. This was cold, sweet, and satisfying. When we'd quenched our thirst, we explored the park together. From that time, I have always loved to commune with nature.

Don and Paul Fujinami (Paul became known as "Little Paul," for obvious reasons) showed me every nook and cranny of the vast expanse that was my new neighborhood. They taught me to capture alligator lizards with a noose made from a blade of grass. When hunger called, we'd catch crawfish in a nearby pond. Don and Paul showed me how to fashion a net made from a wire coat hanger and a nylon stocking. We'd boil them for lunch or head to the nearest farm, taking any produce we desired.

Many farmers were following the trend set by Mr. Fujinami and selling their land to make way for more new homes in the area. Some had left their crops on the vine.

If it were not for the friendship of Don and Paul, I would not have had to courage to pursue a passing dirt devil, then cross into its fifty-foot high vortex, daring it to carry me into the sky. I wouldn't have learned to take time to taste the sweetness of a honeysuckle flower.

Like all country boys, for us, the fun began where the concrete ended. We usually explored on bicycle. Our adventures took us through the open fields and dusty trails known as Rabbit Hill. I remember riding my one-speed Huffy as fast as I could, always searching for a dirt mound to speed over in an attempt to get airborne. Then there was always the dare issued by Don. "Hey, I'll bet you guys won't ride down this."

We'd ease our bikes off a cliff, slide to the bottom with our brakes locked, and then carry our bikes back up the hill to do it again. As far as I knew, this was nothing unique for boys of the '60s. Today, it is referred to as mountain biking.

Eventually, the dirt road was paved and named 190th Street. Our small wilderness soon became the sprawling suburb now known as the City of Carson.

I grew to love Mr. Fujinami. He always spoke to me as if I were one of his sons. One day, he pulled me aside. "Pōru," he called me by my Japanese name. I could see he was troubled. In broken English, he asked whether I wanted to learn judo. With a sad face, he explained that Don and Paul had flatly refused. I noticed early on that Don and Paul seemed ashamed of their culture. We never spoke about it, but I'm sure television destroyed their self-esteem the same way it did with African-Americans. Our favorite television shows dealt with World War II: *12 O'Clock High, The Rat Patrol*, and even comedies like *McHale's Navy* taught us that the Japanese were the enemy.

I was honored that Mr. Fujinami thought so highly of me, and I was not about to disappoint him. Immediately, I agreed to try the sport. After all, what boy wouldn't want to learn martial arts? In my limited experience, every fighting sport associated with the Asian culture was karate. It sounded like the coolest thing in the world. I couldn't wait to learn how to do a real judo chop. Obviously, I did not have the slightest idea what judo was.

Mr. Fujinami took my mother and me to a traditional dojo in Gardena, a predominately Japanese community in the South Bay of Los Angeles. He had a long conversation with the sensei before he introduced me. At the time, I had no idea how groundbreaking this was. He could be, and probably was, ostracized for inviting a black boy to the school. Tradition be damned. Mr. Fujinami was determined to pass on this part of his culture to a family member…or at least a loved one, and it was me. The sensei accepted me, and I became the dojo's first black student.

English was a second language here, but none would speak it to me. There was one Caucasian, an older boy who held a brown belt. He and the sensei were my only friends.

I soon learned there's no such thing as a judo chop. Judo is simply grappling, using holds and leverage to unbalance your opponent or flip him to the ground. I spent the next year of my life learning how to fall. I fell flat on my back, my side, my hands, and my face. Whatever way you can possibly conceive of hitting the ground, I was taught how to absorb the energy of the fall.

I began to love our warm-up regimen, which consisted of stretching every tendon that could be torn, from my little finger, right down to my little toe. Then we practiced falling. We'd start easily, jumping over the smaller kids, who were lined up on all fours on the floor. I could see their fear and dread. I approached, bounded over them, curled into a shoulder roll, slapped the mat on impact, and popped up to my feet. Next, we jumped over the older kids. At least five boys stood side by side, bent at the waist. With a running jump, we were up and over, and ended in a shoulder roll on the other side.

In my second year, I began to develop serious judo techniques. I understood the intent was to train the body and mind. I revered my dojo, and began to embrace Japanese culture. Bowing to show respect for my sensei and dojo became second nature. And I soon found myself bowing to Japanese people outside the dojo. But I still suffered from a language barrier, and could only comprehend the culture through what I saw. I had no idea what was going on at a ceremonial belt promotion ceremony, until the sensei managed to speak three words in English.

"You purple belt."

It came as a complete surprise to me that my first awarded belt was two steps below a black belt. The yellow belt is usually awarded early in the first year of training, and I could dispose of most of the green belts when we sparred. While proud and a bit confused, I got the feeling the sensei was winging it when he got to me.

Judo is quite literally the only sport I ever "outgrew." It was developed in Japan, and brought to America. I was at a distinct disadvantage because of my height. The sport is all about leverage. I became predictable because my height limited me to very few moves. I outgrew the sport, but that is not why left the dojo.

My sensei, who had been so kind to me, went to Japan to study with the masters. The dojo was left to a renegade instructor who had apparently been discharged from other schools for breaking students' arms.

Our replacement sensei was clearly traditional, and I could tell he did not like me. What I mean by that is he clearly did not approve of a *Kuro kokujin* (black) boy in the dojo. He had a scruffy unshaven face and a scratchy, low, somewhat stereotypical-sounding Japanese voice. Immediately, the replacement sensei took a singular interest in choosing me as his sparring partner. I was determined to show him my grit, and did everything in my power to stay on my feet. After being knocked to the mat three or four times with ease, I would arise stronger. I felt frustrated and frightened, but determined nonetheless. Perhaps it was strength from the adrenaline rush of fear. With a tremendous burst of power and bursting *kiai* (a short yell that tenses your solar plexus), I managed to budge my sensei off balance. Sensing he was in trouble, I immediately attacked him by employing Harai Turikomi Ashi (a lifting, pulling, foot sweep). He had a look of absolute horror in his eyes as I struggled to bring him down. He managed to hop on one foot to the edge of the mat before regaining his footing.

"Very good, very good," he growled.

I could tell by his tone that he was impressed with my tenacity.

The next thing I remember was being hurled to the ground with such force that I could not break my fall. All of the dojo looked over when they heard my large thud. Flat on my back, I opened my eyes and attempted to rise. Suddenly, small fireworks began to flash and pop before my eyes. Then a high-pitched sound rang through my ears...*zing, zing, zing*.

I don't know how long I was unconscious. But I knew there was nothing left for me at the dojo without my beloved sensei. This racist had won. He succeeded in running me out of the dojo. But the skills I learned during those two years would come in handy in the strangest place of all. As bizarre as it may sound, one day I would use judo skills on the basketball court.

CHAPTER 5

A WAY WITH WORDS

Some of us are natural-born storytellers, or, as the late CBS newsman Harry Reasoner noted in his memoir, *Before the Colors Fade*:

> Writing talent is basically a built-in thing, like the ability to spin a web in a spider and when it is there and used, it produces that abstraction of experience, that mirror of life which is man's single greatest gift to man.

I've never known where it came from. I do know I began to spin my web in the fourth grade, with little or no help from my teacher. I recall one fourth-grade writing assignment, a fiction piece called "The Last Outpost," utterly oblivious there was a 1951 movie with the same name. It was my first free-form writing experience. I remember developing complex plots and characters with extensive dialogue (as extensive as a fourth-grader's vocabulary could be). In my version, "The Last Outpost" was a long-term shelter buried deep within the earth where a chosen few could survive a nuclear holocaust and ensure the survival of the human race. I've seen the theme repeated on television and in movies and have often wondered where the original copy of my assignment wound up.

I was not an exceptionally gifted student, but I was no dummy either. When we lived in Compton, I was expected to do well in school, and I did that, getting all A's and B's.

But something changed when we moved to Dominguez Hills. Saturated by TV's negative images of Negroes, I considered myself inferior to my new classmates, 95 percent of whom were white. I was part of an entourage from Del Ammo Highlands that integrated Leapwood Avenue Elementary School.

There was no drama when the new Negro students arrived. But while everyone was friendly, I got the feeling that my new teachers didn't expect me to do well. And when I fulfilled that expectation, they were obliged to leave me behind academically. I lacked the fundamentals of written English. Terms like noun, verb, adjective, and pronoun never met at "Conjunction Junction." Their functions were foreign to me. My spelling skills were subpar. Instead of noticing my deficiency and teaching me, my teacher read the front of my notebook, found it amusing, and decided to read it aloud to the entire class. "I hate girls," I thought it proclaimed. It actually read, "I hate grils." I was mortified, and the entire class, including the teacher, was falling out of their seats having a huge laugh at my expense. It was humiliating.

You can blow out a candle, but you can't blow out a fire.
Once the flames begin to catch,
the wind will blow it higher.

— From "Biko," by Peter Gabriel

They say ignorance is bliss. Absent the fundamental building blocks of English, I possessed an extensive vocabulary thanks to radio and television. However, I could not spell half the words I spouted. The narrator inside my young mind relayed images so vividly that time itself could not erase their indelible imprint.

CHAPTER 6

ENERGY

My father was an avid track and field fan. In his youth, he was a distance runner, and so he decided our Boy Scout troop should go to an AAU track meet at the Los Angeles Coliseum. Fully expecting to be bored out of our minds, we were amazed at the plethora of activity on the field before us. As javelins flew, men who resembled Hercules contorted, spun, and, with great screams that could be heard throughout the arena, sent shot-puts flying and discuses soaring. We were immersed in the spectacle, when the sound of gunfire drew our attention from the infield to the track. I looked up in time to see a group of men sprinting away from the starting line. I watched carefully as they rounded the track. To my surprise, they ran slightly off course, off the track surface, to a ramp almost directly in front of us. At the end of the ramp was an open pit filled with water. When the first runner veered off the track, he hurled his body through the air and cleared the pit. The pack followed closely. The last runner mistimed his jump and landed at the edge of the watery pit.

My father explained that this event was the steeplechase, a long-distance endurance event. The three-ring circus distraction of the infield faded. Our eyes were glued on the lead runners as they widened the gap on the pack. The last man seemed to be a pathetic runner. With each passing lap, his distance over the muddy pit shortened, and soon he was landing directly in the water. His shins became muddy. His shoes were no longer white. Soon, instead of cheering for the leaders, we focused on this pathetic athlete and began to boo him as he passed us. Our taunts soon became a personal attack, as we urged him through our jeers to give up. He fell farther behind, as if with each pass before us, we were zapping more of his strength.

During this time, I began to look more closely at the runner. The arena was not full, and perched along the first and second rows of the track, we were by far the most vocal spectators. I studied the runner as his energy level waned. He seemed to dread running past us, and with each lap, not only did he fall farther behind the leader, but also began to miss his jumps altogether and land in the water. What we were doing to him was humiliating, and I knew it. I decided I would no longer be a part of this game. On his next pass, I began to applaud. At that point, Ray Flowers, the main antagonist, stopped his taunts, too. His big brother Steve, who had long since become disgusted with our antics, joined in the applause. On the next lap, something unusual happened: every one of us applauded the last runner. Our applause soon turned to cheers. As he passed, he looked over at us, still last, and still landing in the muddy pit. However, he appeared to run a little faster. Our applause continued as we embraced "our runner." He began to make a move on the back of the pack. When he caught them, we were amazed. When he passed them, we erupted into uncontrollable roars, and his speed increased.

Moments before, we seemed to be able to zap him with our negativity. Now he seemed to be feeding off our positive energy, and we knew it. Soon "our runner" was not only clearing the pit...he was pressing the leaders. Then, several laps later, to our complete amazement, he overtook them and assumed the lead. We became dizzy with excitement as this unlikely runner had not only come from behind, but also had a chance to win the race. Little did we realize that our vocal little group had become the center of attention at this track and field spectacle. We, along with the entire stadium, were on our feet as the bell lap sounded. By now, our runner had amassed an enormous lead over the fading pack. I wondered, "Could this have been his game plan all along...or have we somehow fed this unlikely winner energy to revitalize him and give him the drive to win?" As I pondered the question, he approached us to pass for the last time. He looked up at me, and, with a broad smile on his face, floated over the pit. He then lifted his hand high into the air, turned, and gave us a salute of appreciation as he headed for the finish line. As he crossed the line, my question was answered. Though we were non-participants, we'd clearly had an impact on the outcome of the race, creating what was perhaps the most unlikely victory in steeplechase history.

I came away from that experience with an invaluable lesson about energy. Clearly, there was an invisible force in the universe that I could use anyway I desired. I chose then and there to use it for good. If I possessed a power so great that I could affect the outcome of a race I did not run, just imagine... if it had been *me* in the race.

CHAPTER 7

EVERY GOOD BOY DOES FINE

"Every Good Boy Does Fine," or "E-G-B-D-F,"
is a mnemonic music teachers use to help students
memorize the notes on the lines of the treble clef.

When I entered junior high school, I took up the trumpet. It was not my first choice. The percussion instruments were most popular. It seemed everybody wanted to play the drums, and the section was full. But as it turned out, trumpet was a good fit. With the help of a private instructor and hundreds of hours of practice, my indistinguishable buzzing and squawking, which annoyed everyone in my household, quickly evolved into full-bodied melodic tones. Turns out I had a flair for music; I became an accomplished musician and became the first African American member of the Los Caballeros Youth Band of Carson.

I spent my days with my new best friends, David and Daniel Layne. They were fraternal twins, but they appeared identical. They'd lived right up the street from me for years, but music sealed our friendship with an accent note. David played the trumpet, while Daniel played the cello and guitar. They were a couple of "studious squares." I didn't know them very well until music brought us together. Over time, they would become my most loyal and trusted friends.

Our school was having a talent show, so we formed a band, "The G.R.O.U.P." Acronyms were big at the time. The most notable was the television series *The Man from U.N.C.L.E.*, which stood for United Network Command for Law Enforcement. The G.R.O.U.P. stood for The Groovy Roundabout Outta-Sight Uptown People. Our band consisted of David and me on trumpet, Daniel on electric guitar, our friend and classmate Clarence Broderick, who played the trombone, and a saxophone player named John, whom I'd recruited from my youth band. We also recruited a rockin' drummer who attended our school; his name has escaped me. He owned a full trap set. Our eyes bulged when he unloaded immaculate metallic drums with bright cymbals at our first jam session. "His parents must be loaded," I thought. None of us had seen a drum set like his, except on television. John and our drummer were white. We would lose them to white flight. In 1969, whites were still fleeing integrated neighborhoods in Southern California in droves.

But before our drummer left, and The G.R.O.U.P. disbanded, we all experienced one shining moment of glory together. Clarence's sister was an accomplished seamstress and made our band matching bright-blue African dashikis for the show. I came up with the brilliant idea that we should dance onto the stage, accompanied only by our drummer's funky beat. We settled on the "Temptation Walk," which contained probably the only dance moves I knew. As we strutted onto stage and into view, the standing-room-only crowd erupted into uncontrollable laughter. It was too late to turn tail and hide. We were committed.

After the first riff of the R&B hit "Soul Finger," I knew what it was like to have an audience in the palm of your hand. For one shining evening, we were triumphant rock stars.

I always wondered whether we might have hastened our drummer's departure from Carson. I imagine his parents didn't approve of him hanging out with a group of black boys.

Following the talent show, the Layne brothers and I were rarely apart. In fact, when summer break rolled around the year we entered high school, they invited me to go on vacation with them. They were going island hopping in Hawaii. To my surprise, my mother agreed. We spent three glorious weeks learning the history and culture of the islands, while swimming in every body of water we laid eyes on. At some point during our travels, I dared my friends to follow me off the end of a dock in Maui and then swim to the beach several hundred yards away. It was roughly a twenty-foot plunge, but I decided to be daring and dive in headfirst. I flew into the deep blue water, and surfacing seemed normal. I blew out the stale air in my lungs just before the moment I thought I'd reached the surface, but I soon realized I was much deeper than I'd anticipated. Less buoyant and starving for my next breath, I struggled to surface. When I emerged, I began laughing uncontrollably. I'd never felt so alive. When the twins finally popped up alongside me, we reveled in the moment. Now in the middle of the harbor, we had to swim out of the way of a glass-bottom boat slowly cruising by us. Then I realized the tourists aboard thought we were local kids frolicking in the water. They flocked to the side of the boat to have a closer look. We waved to them and continued to shore. My time in the islands changed the course of my life forever because I seemed to know I would be destined to return one day.

CHAPTER 8

LATE BLOOMER

Late bloomer: *noun* 1. A person whose talents or capabilities are slow to develop.

The term is used metaphorically to describe a child or adolescent who develops more slowly than others in his age group, but eventually catches up and, in some cases, overtakes his peers. The definition fit me to a tee. I was a gangly piece of work. When I look back, I can only describe myself as pathetically skinny. Growing up, my oldest sister likened me to a starving, malnourished African child because my ribs protruded conspicuously from my chest, and my tummy was round, particularly after drinking quarts of water after hard play on hot summer days. Neighborhood kids referred to me as String Bean Beanpole. Girls just called me Goofy.

Imagine growing too fast to consume the sustenance necessary to maintain a healthy body weight. That was my childhood. My feet, which went from acorns to giant oaks, certainly complicated matters. By age ten, my shoe size corresponded directly with my age. At eleven, the tips of my toes began to curl as they pushed against the tips of shoes. Despite my mother's best efforts, new shoes on my feet were like fertilizer to freshly-cut grass during the warmth of spring. You could almost see them growing. No matter what size shoe we purchased, they always seemed to be a half size too small once we left the store.

Despite my ungainly appearance, I possessed uncanny agility. I attributed my coordination to being outdoors all the time and a lifestyle built on the foundation of the Boy Scouts of America. Hiking into remote sections in the wilderness of California, I sprinted up and over riverbeds and across slippery rocks. I jumped from boulder to boulder high atop the cliffs and buttes of Red Rocks Canyon State Park. I'd launch myself off an oceanside cliff with all my strength to land on a sand dune below. I was a kid on the move. Up to that point in my young life, the only organized sport I'd ever participated in was judo, which I'd outgrown.

At 6'5", I began dabbling with the round ball in the ninth grade. A chance happening in my gym class accelerated the process. With a few extra minutes to spare before the close of my junior high Phys-Ed period, our gym teacher posed a question to the class. "Who wants to try to slam dunk this volleyball?" he asked with a broad smile. A volleyball is much smaller in circumference than a basketball and therefore easier to palm or hold with one hand.

This particular gym class happened to be filled with the school's best athletes. The kids he invited to take part in this spectacle were boys in men's bodies. They were behemoths who looked as though puberty had arrived shortly after birth.

We sat expectantly, crossed-legged ("Indian Style," as we used to call it) on the floor in orderly rows.

Glenn Curtis Junior High was new; the gym floor still glistened and smelled of lacquer. I was a member of what would be the first graduating class. And though it was a bit of a cheat with a volleyball versus a basketball, this would still be an historic occasion: The first slam dunks in our new gymnasium.

It was time to break in the floor, to bend the hoops with a thundering dunk, perhaps in the fashion of Wilt "The Stilt" Chamberlain, hero of the Los Angeles Lakers, and, at least to my limited knowledge of the sport at the time, hero to every basketball fan in the world.

"You're up, John," the coach said.

John Wills was a natural athlete, and by far the best basketball player in the school. John wore a huge afro and had leading man good looks. I recall thinking it would take two of my boney legs and perhaps an arm to equal just one of his muscular thighs. "We're about to witness something special," I thought as John easily palmed the ball.

He began the approach without a dribble, walking at first as he sized up the hoop, then accelerating to a full gallop. His massive legs tensed like those of a muscular Greek statue. Suddenly, he shuffled his feet, which stopped his take-off, and ran under the basket.

With a broad smile on his face, our gym coach commanded, "All right, try again."

John eyed his target, meditatively at first, but with a more determined look. The gym grew quiet, as if we were waiting for an Olympian to begin his routine. After a moment, John was ready, and attacked the hoop with full force. This time, he leaped high in the air and took flight as only he could. He rose up and up, and then…THUD, the ball smashed the front of the rim. This pushed John back to a hard landing on his rear, which was quite tragically comic. Come on, you know it's funny when a guy falls on his butt.

Of course, John gave it another go. This time, he made the proper changes in launch trajectory. All of us watching were certain that with this attempt, we would witness history.

THUD.

We did not.

So, with grimaces and unbounded determination, our school's best launched themselves toward the hoop. All flights began with Jordanesque take offs; all also ended with disastrous results as the volleyball bumped the front of the rim and knocked the airborne contestants backwards to a not-so-gentle landing on their collective rear ends.

The boys all took several tries before our coach, who was now chuckling aloud as if he'd already known the outcome, called off the "air show," presumably before someone got hurt.

It became abundantly clear to us that the elusive slam dunk must have been a theoretical impossibility. After all, if the best athletes in all the school couldn't rise to the occasion in front of a gym full of their admiring peers, then clearly it could not be done. End of story.

As the participants in this entertaining endeavor returned to the mortal realm and took seats on the gym floor next to us gym rats, a friend of mine, by the name of Fred Lowe, blurted out, "Let Paul try!"

Now, I'd known Fred since the fourth grade. He'd always been about as tall as I was, but unlike me, he possessed considerable girth, while I remained as thin as a rail. I couldn't gauge the look on his face. I wasn't sure whether he was merely seeking more amusement at my expense...or perhaps trying to humiliate me. Of course, I never once considered a third explanation. Perhaps, just perhaps, Fred knew something about me that I didn't know about myself.

The coach looked at me skeptically, but with about two minutes until the bell, he offered up the ball without comment. I refused, but Fred, with his usual broad smile, urged me to try.

Mortified and embarrassed beyond measure, I grabbed the volleyball in my oversized right hand. I took a quick look at the basket, and in two steps and a hop, it was all said and done. I sent that volleyball ripping through the net with so much force I surprised myself. The gym erupted into ecstatic applause. No one had ever dunked before, even if it was a volleyball. I didn't know another instructor was watching. A few days later, he called my mother at home and asked her to sign me up for a summer basketball camp run by Jerry Tarkanian, head basketball coach at Cal State Long Beach. To my surprise, she did just that.

Jerry Tarkanian, a.k.a. "Tark the Shark," was well on his way to becoming a basketball legend who would construct some of the finest teams in NCAA history. He put the lowly Long Beach State University 49ers on the map, while changing the landscape of the game by placing Edward Ratleff at point guard. Ratleff, a member of the 1972 U.S. Olympic basketball team, was the sport's first "super guard." The nearly 6'7" Ratleff was as tall as any power forward of the day, but could handle the ball as well as any point guard in the land.

Though his shorter counterparts could not contend with him on defense, opposing coaches were unwilling to make the adjustment. The towering anomaly was too quick outside to be guarded by forwards and too tall for guards to contend with his jump shot.

Under Tark's tutelage, Ed Ratleff forced coaches to abolish the unwritten rule that big men could not, should not, dribble. He almost single-handedly evolved the game of basketball and was a predecessor to players like Magic Johnson and Larry Bird.

Ratleff was a no show at the summer basketball camp I attended. I was taught basic skills by members of the Long Beach State coaching staff, as Tark the Shark looked on.

Suddenly, West Coast basketball became more than the UCLA dynasty. Following Long Beach State's first appearance in the 1970 NCAA tournament, the running debate in Southern California was which was the better team, the 49ers or the Bruins?

The great UCLA coach John Wooden refused to schedule a regular-season game with the 49ers, but our burning question would be answered in 1971 when UCLA and Long Beach State met in the NCAA's Western Regional final. Long Beach State led by 12 points at half time, but in the end, UCLA prevailed 57 to 55.

By then, thousands of new homes surrounded our tiny subdivision. In 1969, the area which had been known as Dominguez Hills was incorporated into the City of Carson. The original Rancho Dominguez was steeped in history, dating back to California's first Spanish land grant. In 1968, residents voted to name the area Carson, after the local high school, essentially erasing 100 years of history.

Carson High, just four miles away from my house, was predominantly white. Somehow, the L.A. Unified School District, in all its wisdom, refused to integrate it. Instead, it shipped students from my neighborhood out of the city to Phineas Banning High School in Wilmington, near the Port of Los Angeles. At the time, Banning was primarily Hispanic, with a large Pacific Island population. The school was overcrowded, so the district moved bungalows to the campus to accommodate the influx of new students. Meanwhile, the main campus was in the beginning stages of demolition to make way for a new school. While desperately needed, everyone I knew assumed the improvements to Banning were a way to keep minorities out of Carson.

The Layne brothers and I were not interested in politics, only music. Gardena High School had the best music program in the L.A. Unified School District. Besides music, the predominately-Japanese high school was noted for academics. The combination made it most desirable for anyone who valued education. Since the twins were already planning to attend Gardena, I decided to try to dodge Banning High, the neglected facility overrun with bungalows.

We entered the district lottery to attend Gardena and won.

On the first day of school, we lined up outside in a quad area to meet with our counselors. Mine took a moment to gaze up from his paperwork. Setting his eyes upon me for the first time, he immediately announced, "You're on the basketball team." I had grown nearly an inch over the summer and was approaching 6'7" tall.

"Why the heck not?" I remember thinking. After all, I had almost two full weeks of training under my belt from summer basketball camp. As long as I was able to play in the band and orchestra, everything else Gardena had to offer was a bonus as far as I was concerned.

By the middle of the first term, Gardena's legendary music department was coming apart at the seams. Our illustrious director, whom we affectionately referred to as Mr. Ed (short for Edmondson), had vanished. Before long, we learned an undercover narcotics officer posing as a student had busted him for selling marijuana on campus. He never returned to school. We were devastated.

The district's plum teaching assignment was awarded to an elderly music teacher from Washington High. Washington had a less than sterling reputation on pretty much all fronts back then. Sadly, our new director dropped the baton, so to speak, and the band and orchestra floundered from its all-city band status. I was at that high school for the sole purpose of playing in the best band and orchestra in the city, which became one of the worst.

At the time, Gardena High School was a perennial football powerhouse out of the then-Marine League of the Los Angeles Unified School District. For Gardena, winning a city championship was commonplace. Basketball, on the other hand, was an afterthought. Anything better than last place in the league was considered a successful season.

Based solely on my height, I was a member of the basketball team. It remained to be seen whether I could actually play the sport. As I chased a group of players down the court during a fast break, I suppose my coach saw something special.

Three players directly in front of me collided, and two fell to the ground. Running at full gait, I leapt over the pile. In the tangle, someone caught my foot just enough to throw me off balance, and I was airborne. I flew ten feet, soaring like Superman, seconds before a hard crash to the floor. I simply tucked and rolled, like I'd done thousands of times in judo class. Without missing a beat, I popped to my feet and continued down court as if nothing had ever happened.

My agility, or should I say the ability to avoid calamity, amazed the coach. That single acrobatic flash of coordination elevated me on the team's depth chart, which turned out to be a blessing and a curse. A young point guard named Tony Prescott was sitting next to the coach when I performed my flying shoulder roll. He was impressed and became determined to make me his new best friend, and he seemingly never left my side.

Our team was preparing to face Banning High School. I was going to start on the junior varsity. I had never been so excited to play in a basketball game. We were inside Banning's gym warming up when my coach pulled me aside. "Paul," said Coach Panovtich, "we may need your help tonight on varsity."

So I watched our JV game from the bench, as all my friends from the neighborhood looked on.

When it was time for the varsity game, I sat pensively on the bench. During the course of that game, the coach would approach and study me. At one point, he walked in front of me and said, "Get ready to go in."

The moment I began to take off my sweats, he held me in place by lifting his hand in the stop motion.

It was one of the most disappointing nights of my young life since I never entered the game. My coach explained after the fact that once I entered the floor as a varsity player, I could not return to the junior varsity team. He explained that he wanted me to get lots of playing time on the JV team, rather than sitting the bench on varsity. I'm sure the boys from Banning simply thought I was still Goofy Paul.

One year and one inch later, leading the junior varsity team paid off. At 6'8" in height, I was excelling. My team had become a respectable power in the Marine League thanks to Mike Stevens, a 6'8" senior, and me. UCLA and Milwaukee Bucks great Marcus Johnson (whom we faced when we played Crenshaw High) referred to us as the original twin towers. Suddenly, Gardena High School basketball games filled the gym with spectators. I began to love the sport, but my passion was still music.

One evening after a basketball game, I showered and headed straight to the band room for the annual Christmas concert. Our principal pulled double duty and congratulated me on the win. He was surprised to see me in the auditorium and impressed that I would attend the concert after such a grueling game.

After my solos on the trumpet and French horn, I think it is safe to say he was mesmerized. It was only then I realized that when he'd greeted me earlier, he had no idea I was a member of the orchestra.

When he approached me after the concert, he looked at me as if I'd changed his life. I will never forget the look of pride on his face. It was as if he were meeting me for the first time. He was unbelievably happy I was a student at his high school.

Now, I am 100 percent sure there is a way to turn that lovely encounter into a joke. Fortunately, Tony Prescott, my devoted friend and teammate, was not present.

CHAPTER 9

THE DATING GAME

Tony Prescott's sharp tongue and wit never failed to bring a smile to my face. He could easily diminish the tension of any court blunders with nonsensical comic one-liners that would usually bring the team to its knees with laughter.

"Paul," he would say, "You're so tall... if snow was black, you'd be a walking blizzard." Tony was good with words that way.

He was the all-time champion of a game we called "The Dozens." For your edification, the *Urban Dictionary* describes "The Dozens" as "an African-American custom in which two opponents—usually males—go head to head in a competition of comic trash talk. They take turns cracking on or insulting one another, their adversary's mother, or family members, until one of them has no comeback."

Tony Prescott always had a comeback. "Yo Mama's so fat she's gotta grease the tub to take a bath," he would say. The team would crumble into uncontrollable laughter.

I listened contently, putting most of Tony's lines in my arsenal for later use. Oddly enough, one of the best would land me a date. Not just any date, but a "Dating Game" dream double date.

"From Hollywood, it's *The Dating Game* with your host, Jim Lange," the announcer would proclaim as trumpets blared the catchy theme song. *The Dating Game*, an ABC television show, first aired in 1965. Three eligible bachelors (or bachelorettes) sat hidden from view from an eligible bachelorette (or bachelor), who asked them a series of questions and then chose one of the three for a date.

Daniel Layne applied to be on the show, and they asked him to bring friends along for the audition. Since we were as thick as thieves, I went along for the ride. We all had fun playing a practice version of the game. Since contestants had to be eighteen years old (I was still seventeen), I fudged my age. No one ever checked it, and to my utter disbelief, I received a call saying I'd been chosen to be on the show. Oddly enough, Daniel was chosen to be on the same show with me. We received specific instructions on how to dress and when to arrive. Somehow, I managed to get the instructions wrong. They told us that we were *not* to wear white shirts, and that's exactly what I wore. I mention this because the host, Jim Lange, graciously went into his wardrobe and let me borrow one of his shirts. The fit was pretty darn close.

Once on stage, the tables turned to reveal three eligible bachelors. Daniel was designated bachelor number one; I was bachelor number two. And there was bachelor number three, a guy too cool for school. He was a handsome, browned-skinned smooth talker with all the lines. This dude exuded confidence and sounded like a playboy. I assumed he would be the winner after he answered the first question.

The bachelorette was Cheryl Davis, an attractive black girl from an inner-city high school. Back then, there was no crossing the color line—especially on television. Cheryl began asking her silly questions (which I later found out were written by *The Dating Game* staff).

"Bachelor number three," she said in a cute squeaky voice. "There are boys, there are men, and there are dudes. But you're Super Dude. How would you describe your outfit?"

"Well, my outfit is blue," he said, going on to describe the intricacies in the fabric's design as a way to chew up time. "On the front it has an S, and on the back there's a sign that reads, 'When you passed me by, Baby, you just missed out.'"

How cool was that? Super Cool, check and mate! "Game over," I thought.

"Bachelor number one, my favorite singer is Diana Ross. In the voice of my favorite singer, sing what you are going to teach me on our date." Daniel replied with a goofy comeback, singing "I love you" in a high, drawn-out tone. Cheryl laughed nervously.

"How about you, bachelor number two?"

Caught off guard, I said, "First of all," and then spouted out my best Diana Ross imitation, "I'll get you back in my arms again." The crowd got a kick out of it, and I could hear Cheryl laughing.

The game progressed, and Cheryl asked, "Bachelor number one and bachelor number two, bachelor number three is a girl. Describe the way she looks."

Daniel charged right in with, "Golly, she sure is fine. Just look at her."

I sat silently as Jim Lange interrupted. "How about you, bachelor number two?"

I was so nervous. I hadn't realized I was included in the question, but quickly harped in. "Hey now...lookin' pretty good." Not wanting to compliment him, I was able to pull a Tony Prescott line out of my butt and said, "She's got a little butter, but no biscuit." The crowd went wild.

"Thank you, Tony Prescott," I thought.

Daniel and I sat quietly during the commercial break, both complimenting bachelor number three in advance of winning the date.

"Welcome back to *The Dating Game*," said Jim Lange. He gave the rundown of the terrific trio of bachelors and said, "Cheryl, which one will it be? Bachelor number one, bachelor number two, or bachelor number three?"

"Bachelor number two," she announced.

"What did you like about bachelor number two?" asked Jim Lange.

"I liked the way he sang," she answered.

That was what she said on television. On our date, she confessed that she thought bachelor number three sounded like an arrogant playboy. And Tony's line slapped him down. Tony's line won me the date.

It was my first time on television, and I liked it. Little did I know it would not be my last.

Cheryl and I saw each other a couple of times after our "Dating Game" date, but she was soon off to college at Texas Christian University, and I, the big Dating Game fibber, was sailing into my senior year of high school.

CHAPTER 10

WILLIE BARNES

Somewhere along the way, my friend Tony broke his arm in three places. If you observed him closely, you could tell his right arm was a tad shorter than his left. This injury proved to be a major asset on the basketball court, as his altered bone structure resembled the prototypical perfect jump shot. With his arms extended, Tony's release was an art form. When he got hot, good things usually followed.

Tony lost his mind in a game against Carson High. Our team was on a hot streak, in which we'd defeated every team in the league. After connecting on his first two field goals, he cast our game plan to the wind and started to fire at will. After his third, then fourth long-range shots (which in today's game would be considered three pointers), he began to laugh. As our eyes met, he shrugged his shoulders as if to say, "I'm having an out-of-body experience." Or to put it simply, "When you're hot, you're hot!" As he turned to fall back to defense, it looked as though he was dancing on air. Tony single-handedly defeated Carson that evening. It was a fun time in the Marine League.

After the game, we planned to go out and celebrate. But unlike me and the other members of the team, Tony had other obligations. He held a part-time job at Kentucky Fried Chicken to help make ends meet at home. On most Friday nights, I would faithfully wait for my friend in the parking lot of a KFC in South Central Los Angeles, knowing I'd be rewarded for the wait. Tony never left without at least a bucket of fried chicken in hand.

My car was full of teammates and Tony, who took the window rear seat, brought enough chicken for everyone. I happily gorged myself as I'd done so many times before. Tony suggested we cruise the Sunset Strip and check out the scene in Hollywood. As we rolled down a side street for a return trip down the Strip, I spotted a beautiful woman. Tony pulled down the window and abruptly blurted out, "Hey, I'll bet you got a big ol' dick in those pants."

I was in utter shock and thought Tony had lost his mind. Suddenly, this gorgeous creature shouted back, "Fuck you!" She had the vocal tenor of a burly man.

Unbeknownst to me, we were cruising in an area frequented by transvestites. Obviously, Tony had been there before, and seemed to take great joy in getting these men to break character, so to speak. I couldn't contain my laughter as I sped away. To my knowledge, I'd never seen a transvestite.

A few minutes later, while roaming the area on foot, I heard a familiar voice call out my name. "Paul. Paul Jackson? Is that you?"

I slowly turned and, to my dismay, there at a corner bus stop was Willie Barnes, the only openly gay person I knew. Willie lived a block down the street from us. He was a rotund individual whom, to the best of my recollection, resembled Fat Albert. He was dressed in a loose-fitting outfit, which might have been colorful pajamas. He clutched a woman's purse. Taking his left hand from his hip, he flipped his wrist downward, as if to announce publicly he was a flaming homosexual.

I was mortified. My first impulse was to turn and rush away.

Willie and my older sister were friends in high school. They were in several school plays together, so Willie was at our house on a regular basis, practicing lines, or just hanging out like one of the girls. Until then, I'd always found him uncomfortably amusing. He was vociferous and appeared to be an exceedingly happy person. I also considered him a talented actor, who never failed to light up the stage. You know, the kind of actor who made you believe Harvey was actually standing next to him.

"Oh...look at you, boy," he said flirtatiously. "You look good."

I could hear my teammates laughing a few feet away. I forced a smile and greeted him as I would any family friend. He immediately began to gush over me, repeating how wonderful I looked. Then he added, "You are really growing up," as his flirtation continued.

Though it all seemed quite creepy, I graciously endured his compliments while doing my level best to keep a smile on my face. I engaged him in friendly banter about my family. All the while, I felt deeply embarrassed to be talking to this freak on Hollywood Boulevard.

As I rejoined my teammates, I turned to look back at Willie and suddenly felt sad and ashamed. I'd already felt uneasy about harassing the transvestites in the area. And when Willie shouted out my name, I knew that by association, I was in for the ribbing of a lifetime from my teammates. Yet to me, the choice was simple. Seeing Willie standing so alone and awkward on the street corner on that Friday night in 1973 was a defining moment for me.

With my teammates still taunting, I slowly turned and walked back toward Willie, my mind flooded with thoughts. It just wasn't right to disavow a friend because he was gay.

Moreover, gay bashing was wrong, I thought. Yes, Willie was a sissy, but he had the kindest heart of anyone I knew and (at least to my knowledge) never hurt a soul.

"It was really good to see you, Willie," I said, looking deep into his eyes. "You take care of yourself." Inwardly, I realized this dear, sweet man was my friend, and I was afraid his flamboyant appearance might land him in serious trouble. Many homosexuals were beaten during this era. It was referred to as gay bashing.

"Oh Paul, you are really growing up," said Tony, with his hand on his hip, trying his best to imitate Willie's feminine mannerisms.

I thought to myself, "Perhaps I am... Perhaps I am."

CHAPTER 11

THREE-MINUTE MILE

SOME THINGS ARE IMPOSSIBLE. There is no explanation for what happened. Against all odds, it simply did. Forget the fact it was an utter impossibility. Get my drift? I have such stories.

My sister Elizabeth thought she knew exactly how each and every member of the family should live his or her life, and would do all in her power to bend that vision to her will. This mostly involved emotional diatribes to my mother about what a spoiled little punk I was. She was of the opinion that I needed to be hardened.

She tried to convince my mother I needed to switch high schools and attend Verbum Day, an all-boy Catholic school just off South Central Avenue, smack-dab in the middle of Watts. The school's basketball teams were proverbial California Interscholastic Federation (CIF) champions. Being a member of the team virtually guaranteed an athletic scholarship to the college of your choice. Just two problems: Number one, the whole Watts thing, which in itself terrified me, as I envisioned getting gunned down or knifed on the way to school. And two, the last thing on my agenda was being separated from the opposite sex during my high school years. That was simply not an option.

After successfully fighting off months of urging from my weak-minded mother, who always seemed to agree with Elizabeth, I remained at Gardena.

One day, Elizabeth met and befriended the head coach of the Washington High School basketball team. They went on a couple of dates. Soon, I became part of their romantic entanglement. I first met him in the hallway of our home. He was young and rotund; in fact, at first glance, I thought he was a football coach. I could tell he was trying to mask his amazement at my size as I came loping out of the narrow hallway with the ceiling just inches from my head. After an awkward introduction, he began to play right into my sister's theme of me not being all I could be at Gardena. It was as if he were reading from a script.

"You need to play for me," he said.

What he didn't realize was that I knew Washington High was the doormat of the league at the time because they needed size.

This guy called me day and night, and teamed with Elizabeth to trap me at home for chats. Finally, I agreed to visit Washington for an unofficial try-out.

Have you ever had a feeling that you just don't belong somewhere? That uneasy feeling fell over me the moment I arrived outside the Washington campus. It was a dreary, rundown place. I knew I did not want to be there even before I got out of the car to head for the gym. Nonetheless, I had to follow through on my agreement to visit. When I walked across campus, I fought the physically sick feeling you get in the pit of your stomach when you are frightened. I met the coach in the gym, and he put me through some basic skills tests before walking me to the track to meet the other coaches.

He introduced me to the track coach, who asked me to run a mile. By then, I was exploding with internal turmoil over how I'd let things get this far. I wanted to leave in the worst way, so I began to look for a way out.

The coach stood, stopwatch in hand, and it was pretty much, *on your mark, get set... go!* And that's exactly what I did. I sprinted as hard as I could, trying to exercise my nervous energy. Football players were on the field, watching this outsider from Gardena take their field, and that frightened me even more. I wondered whether they would have jumped and pummeled me without a coach present.

"I should not be here," I kept thinking. As I sprinted, I imagined the hounds of hell were hot on my heels. On my second lap, I noticed other coaches had joined the track coach to find out who this tall lanky kid speeding around the track was. With all eyes on me, I ran even faster. Eventually, I overcame what runners call the wall, and my pain gave way to pleasing endorphins. Suddenly, I felt like I could run not only faster, but forever. As I passed the coach for my third and final lap, his jaw dropped as I continued faster than when I began.

When the mile was over, I remember being disappointed. "Now I will have to face the crowd, and worse, talk to the coaches," I thought.

Staring down at his stopwatch, the coach said in a befuddled voice, "Ever run track?" His face was awash with a look of disbelief.

"No," I answered, and with that, I left the high school. I knew I'd run faster than I had ever run in my life, but I didn't understand the implications of what I had done.

At the tender age of seventeen, without so much as a warm-up, I had run a world class time. True, I was 6'8"—the son of a track star and in fantastic shape. I often went for long runs on the beach from Manhattan to Malibu and back. But if his stopwatch were in any way accurate, I truly missed my calling. I'd just breezed through a sub-four mile (3:58:9), seconds off a world record pace.

Not possible? Impossible things happen every day. In this case, I refer to it as the adrenaline factor. Looking back, I realize I was being chased by fear. And in my estimation, I out-ran it.

As a 6'9" senior, I led Gardena to its first winning season. We came within one game of the city playoffs, and beat every team in the league at least once. I was voted the team's most valuable player. Despite my success, coaches snubbed me and named me to the Marine League's second team.

This designation upset my coach much more than it did me. In fact, he took it as an affront to his coaching abilities. Coach Mickey Panovitch was intensely apologetic when he informed me of the league's decision, adding that coaches debated my status the entire meeting. He never gave me the details of their debate. But in retrospect, I figured out that Banning's coach was punishing me for not attending my designated school. Nonetheless, it was one of the happiest times in my life. Offers for athletic scholarships were rolling in left and right. One particular offer was not on the books.

My coach loved me more than I knew. He wanted to send a message to the coaches in the league that they shouldn't have disrespected him or me. "You can attend UCLA on a full scholarship," he told me.

I was stunned. Panovitch had asked his college coach, the greatest coach in the land, for a favor. And John Wooden, the Wizard of Westwood, gladly obliged. I had an opportunity to play for one of the greatest basketball coaches in the history of the sport. Without a moment to contemplate what was being offered, I gave my answer: No.

I felt I wasn't good enough, and I wanted to play for a team that wanted me. I didn't want to be a favor. I wanted to play where I could make a difference. Most of all, I wanted to play. In my mind, I could pretty much count on a spot on the UCLA bench. I didn't want to be the player the fans cheered for getting off the pine during the closing minutes of the game.

Besides, I thought, I had no less than twenty-one offers to attend colleges that wanted me, and I knew exactly where I wanted to go: The University of Hawaii. The weeks I'd spent exploring the islands with the Laynes planted the seed. I'd followed the Rainbows ever since. In fact, I was not the least bit surprised when I began to receive recruiting letters from the team, an up-and-coming force in the NCAA.

With my decision made, I simply waited for my offer. I waited and waited, but the offer never arrived. Frustrated, I called the basketball office and left a message. "This is Paul Jackson from Gardena High. You've been sending me letters for two years, and I want to come," I told the answering machine. There was no return call.

Two days later, the principal popped his head into my history class. "Can I speak to Paul Jackson for a moment?" he asked.

It is not good when the principal pulls you out of class. What could I have done?

"Paul, I'd like you to meet Bruce O'Neil from the University of Hawaii," he said with a smile.

O'Neil flashed a knowing smile. He was a tall man, one of the youngest NCAA Division 1 coaches at the time.

I happened to be wearing my high-heeled boots (high fashion for men in the early '70s), which made me appear to be seven feet tall.

"We'd like to have you at the University of Hawaii," he said. "We can fly you out to take a look."

Without so much as a breath of hesitation, I replied. "No, that's okay," I said, then added, "I've been there."

Duh…

First, I'd turned down a full ride to UCLA, and now an all-expense trip to visit Hawaii.

C'est la vie (such is life). Or lack of life experience.

CHAPTER 12

HAWAII 5-0

In the summer of 1973, I packed my bags and headed to Hawaii on a full basketball scholarship.

It was an extraordinary time for the University of Hawaii's men's basketball team. The year before I arrived, a group of players known as the "Fabulous Five" carried the Rainbows to the school's first NCAA tournament. All-American John Pennybacker, Bob Nash, Al Davis, Jerome Freeman, Dwight Holiday, and coach Red Rocha had an astonishing 24-2 run. Just like that, the Aloha State was in the national spotlight.

Coach Rocha had retired, leaving the program to Bruce O'Neil, at the time the youngest coach in the NCAA. I was recruited in to build on that success.

The "Honolulu Star Bulletin" lauded the arrival of the late bloomer from Gardena High School. The athletic department listed my height at a whopping 6' 11", the tallest player in the history of the University of Hawaii. But truth was I was 6' 9 ½". In their defense, I was still growing like a weed.

The University of Hawaii was a happening place. I could devote an entire book to describing the clarity of the ocean, color of the sky, and warmth of the people, without fully relating its beauty. Mere words cannot describe this island paradise. You must personally experience that first kiss of a warm trade wind touched by the scent of orchids and pikake flowers to comprehend its exquisiteness.

The state didn't have any professional teams. Therefore, we had superstar status. I was flabbergasted the first time I rode my bicycle away from my Manoa Valley apartment when a little Japanese boy ran beside me, excitedly yelling, "There's Paul Jackson! There's Paul Jackson! Hi, Paul Jackson!"

Uncomfortable with my instant celebrity, I waved and continued.

Little did I know that we were bigger stars on the Island than Don Ho. I was famous, lived in an island paradise, and had yet to play in a single basketball game. With fame came groupies. Local girls loved basketball players.

I hadn't had much luck with girls in high school, other than my experience on *The Dating Game*. Without exception, high school girls rejected my advances. During my senior year, Gretchen, a skinny sophomore, became enamored with me. It so happened that I looked up to her big brother, Mark, who was a starter on Gardena's varsity basketball team when I was a sophomore. The 6'5" forward was the team captain, a leader who often took me aside and offered me tips to improve. He always treated me with the utmost respect.

Gretchen played the clarinet. If you're not familiar with bands, the woodwind section generally sits in front of the brass section. Anytime we stopped playing, Gretchen would turn around and gaze at me. She was a tall girl of Dutch descent. She had blonde hair, a golden tan, and a quick smile.

Soon, I began to see her on campus every time I turned around. I quickly surmised she was stalking me. I was a bit uncomfortable with being her prey. My eyes were still set on long-time crushes, whom I tried repeatedly to ask out. They all did their best to let me down easy, but the black girls wanted nothing to do with me. Oddly enough, the girls I adored most were both daughters of politicians.

There was Keta, whose father was the mayor of Compton. I'd had a crush on her since I was a child. Our families were acquainted through Jack and Jill of America, an organization for young African Americans. And there was Ruthie, the daughter of a well-known California State Representative. She was a tall, thin girl with flawless light brown skin, a pleasing face, and beautiful flowing hair. Neither would offer me the time of day.

I'm not sure what finally set in first, reality or loneliness, but it became clear that I was wasting my time pursuing them. Plus, a beautiful young girl was pursuing me! And so, Gretchen and I began dating.

In public, I felt uneasy having a white girlfriend. In those days, folks were quick to do double takes, and many gave us disapproving stares. But Gretchen was a wonderful girl who loved me, and she was my first true love.

Gretchen kept our relationship a secret from her family for quite some time. We met secretly every weekend to spend our evenings in a lovers' embrace. Ah, young love, perfecting our kissing methods and learning to avoid each other's braces. If you've ever locked braces with another person, then you know what a uniquely horrifying, yet oddly gratifying, experience it can be.

When I finally met Gretchen's mother, she was mortified. Gretchen's father was an LAPD homicide detective. "You don't understand," she told me nervously. "He will kill you if he finds out."

At the time, I thought her mother was simply exaggerating to keep me away from her daughter. I realized she was speaking the truth after Gretchen's father retired from the police force, left his family, and moved to Idaho, presumably to live with members of the Aryan Nation.

When I left for Hawaii, Gretchen and I assured each other we would stay together. But she grew more beautiful, and became the object of attention for nearly every boy in high school. And so it was that the ocean between us did not make our hearts grow fonder. Instead, it made our hearts forget.

I was no longer monogamous. In fact, two words described me best: Hawaiian playboy. It seemed the foreign exchange students from China and Japan were eager to immerse themselves in new cultures.

My days on the island of Oahu were spent either bodysurfing or exploring Manoa Valley, where the university was located. I occasionally attended lectures, but only to scope out the pretty girls. At night, I partied in Honolulu and Waikiki Beach. The drinking age was eighteen, and wherever I went, drinks were on the house. I became such a regular at nightclubs in the international marketplace that bands would announce my arrival. It was a surreal experience for an eighteen-year-old just out of high school.

After living a life most people can only dream of, reality struck me down when I received my first report card. But let me back up here. I'd heard somewhere that basketball players got a free pass. Not in my case. My days of cutting class in favor of bodysurfing at Makapuu Point hit me right between the eyes. I got two D's, one C, and an F. That's a 0.5 GPA, if you're counting. The NCAA placed me on academic probation.

One D grade was in a world religions class. D, of course, stands for barely passing, but I got more out of that class than any letter representing a grade would ever demonstrate. My parents were devout Episcopalians. Indoctrinated as a child, I followed their faith blindly, believing it was the only truth. The only true God was *our* God.

What I was able to surmise from my world religions class was that virtually everyone said the same thing, but in a slightly different way. I was enlightened! Feeling very clever, I decided to change. Instead of saying, "May the Lord be with you," as I had been taught to say from the moment I could speak, I changed a single word to reflect my new worldview. The word "Lord" became "Force." I recall being pleased with my clever new terminology. Whenever I got the chance, I went about the island spouting to friends, "May the Force be with you."

Perhaps, just perhaps, George Lucas was on vacation in the islands at the time. Or maybe choosing to say Force instead of Lord was a natural progression that thousands of people figured out long before I did. I do know that when *Star Wars* became a worldwide theater phenomenon some years later, I was both excited and disappointed. I could no longer use my blessing with the same conviction. Nor would anyone believe I'd coined the phrase years before the Jedi Knights used it.

My lone C grade was in Freshman English. The young professor was a *haole* (the Hawaiian word for a person who is not a native Hawaiian, especially a Caucasian) from the mainland. The boys in my class were local (with the exception of foreign exchange students from the Far East), and worshiped her as the epitome of beauty.

"This was one class I will never cut," I recall one of the boys saying. Apparently, among Asian students, my English teacher was a goddess, but whatever they saw in her was lost on me. She didn't give a lot of homework. Perhaps that's why I was in her class.

One day, she gave us a take-home writing assignment. I don't recall the topic, but it interested me very much. I wanted to write something I could be proud of, and I wanted it to be spelled correctly. So I took my time, and used a dictionary. This was long before the advent of computerized spell check.

A few days after I turned in the assignment, I was called to the office of the assistant men's basketball coach. Peering over his desk with a grin on his face, he pulled out my paper and tossed it onto his desk.

"Okay, who wrote this?"

I smiled, thinking it was a joke. "I did," I replied.

"Really. Who wrote it?" It was not a joke.

It took some time to convince the coach that I'd actually written my own English paper. The next day, I tracked down the professor and explained that I was the true author of my story. I confessed I was a horrible speller and had actually taken time to use a dictionary for the assignment.

From then on, when she looked at me, she would no longer see the tallest basketball player in University of Hawaii history, a student whom she thought illiterate. Rather, she'd see a talented freshman, a natural-born conveyor of the human condition. She would see a writer…and a damn good one at that.

That single assignment turned a failing grade into a C+.

I suppose I began to view her in a different light after that. I realized my classmates were right after all. With her bright smile now directed at me, she was hot.

At that time in my life, I suppose I was a bit of an anomaly, still happily existing in both the world of music and athletics. I had the University of Hawaii Orchestra in my sights. This group consisted of the best collegiate musicians in Hawaii.

I sensed a little more than skepticism from the orchestra's conductor when I entered the music department to introduce myself. A tiny Japanese man, who barely took time to look up at me, was inside doing paperwork. He assumed I was lost and asked why I was there.

"I want to join the orchestra," I informed him. He was clearly taken aback.

Without inquiring about my background, he said, "You mean *band*."

"No, orchestra," I told him.

"What do you play?"

"Trumpet."

"The orchestra is fairly advanced. You should join the marching band," he insisted.

"No. I want to join the orchestra."

Now clearly annoyed, he barked, "Membership in the orchestra is by audition only," then added, "and freshmen are rarely accepted."

I got the feeling he didn't like me much. I thought, *He's probably thinking, "Why is this clueless jock bothering me? He doesn't belong in our orchestra."*

Despite our contemptuous back and forth, I decided I would not heed his advice, but would instead audition for a seat in the orchestra. Begrudgingly, he scheduled my audition for the following afternoon.

I don't remember the piece I played, but it felt familiar. I sight-read the music, and it flowed with comfort and ease. No mistakes. I will never forget the look of disbelief on the conductor's face. Then he showed me a broad smile. "We practice every afternoon at three," he told me.

I was in. I'd accomplished what other freshmen could not, and I would become (to my knowledge) the first African American member of the University of Hawaii Orchestra.

Practice every afternoon at three, I thought to myself. *Practice every afternoon at three....*

Disappointment began to well up inside me. *Three o'clock,* I thought. *That's when the basketball team practices.*

I had come to Hawaii by way of a full athletic scholarship. My choice was clear. I set aside my trumpet and memory of EGBDF and replaced it with NCAA Division 1.

A few days later, my disappointment turned to an enormous sense of pride and accomplishment, when assistant Coach Jim Halm summoned me to his office. "I hear you like music," he said unexpectedly. "Here. This is for you." Then he handed me season tickets to the Honolulu Symphony Orchestra.

It later dawned on me where the tickets had come from. Through my command of music, I had left an impression on the university's conductor. Perhaps I'd changed the way he perceived athletes…especially tall, black ones. Perhaps I was breaking down stereotypes.

Any warm, fuzzy feeling I had about UH hardened the first time I walked onto the basketball court. Before I joined the ranks of the NCAA, I held its athletes in the highest regard. They were, or so I thought, the best of the best. Clean-cut, young men who possessed strength, honor, and, above all, sportsmanship. It was a pleasant fantasy.

I led a sheltered life in high school. Gardena resembled the real-world United Nations. The student population mirrored the cultural richness of the world. Asians were the majority, followed by other people of color. Whites were the minority. Everyone seemed to get along. It was a safe place where students talked to each other, a place where disagreements never came to fisticuffs.

That said, on one occasion, I used a judo technique to flip a fellow student to the gym floor after an altercation got out of hand. The head football coach gave us swats, and then sent us about our day. I would have thought nothing of the scuffle, but the following day, one of the captains of the basketball team, who happened to be Japanese, approached me.

"I saw you flip that guy," said Darryl Otsu, giving me a disenchanted look. He didn't need to say a single word more. I got the message through non-verbal communication, and through his look of disappointment. We are Gardena. Martial arts are for sport. We don't fight here.

Playing basketball in Hawaii was different. I'd never encountered hard-core thugs firsthand until I faced Melton

Wartz, a twenty-two-year-old monster from an East Coast prep school.

Wartz was one of the biggest guys I'd ever seen. He was 6'8," and seemed to be on the other side of 300 pounds. This wide-body was Hawaii's starting center. He had dark skin and wore a big Afro. His arms were freakishly long and muscular, which allowed him to play like he was seven feet tall.

The jump shot, which served me so well in high school, was useless against him. The first time he blocked it, I thought it was an aberration. The second time, I was flat-out embarrassed. Because I was a newcomer, he viewed me as a threat, so he immediately set out to establish his dominance.

After that, every time I scrimmaged against him, I thought, *Yes, today is a good day to die.* I battled hard with no fear, but because of the size difference, when we made contact, and it happened often, I was on the receiving end of a bruising. In boxing terms, it was like a featherweight sparring with a super-heavyweight.

But there are two sides to every coin, and UH coaches apparently liked the qualities I possessed. Despite Wartz's awesome might, I could jump a little higher and move a bit faster. I quickly developed a strategy that if I couldn't go through him, I'd have to go over him, which I did often. Our close encounters created friction. Wartz was of a mind to swat this annoying gnat continually buzzing about him. With brute force, he employed the laws of physics. The smaller mass (me) went flying. By the time I picked myself up, he was already down the court, waiting with a smug look. His intent was transparent. He was trying to terrorize me. Worse yet, he was trying to punk me out.

Then it was my turn. I flew down the court with fury in my eyes, intending to front him, post up, and take him to the hoop. *Whoop!* I never saw that right cross coming, but I certainly have the scar under my chin to remember it by.

Suddenly, the Boy Scout in me woke up. "What did you do that for?" I asked, with blood gushing from my chin. I thought about retaliation, but I quickly concluded that an all-out assault against him would be futile. I didn't think I had enough power to do any meaningful damage.

Wartz stood there, staring at me, stunned. It was clear he thought I intended to attack him.

"Our ball," I said angrily. I hardened my game that day, battling to a bloody—and I do mean bloody—conclusion. I never showed fear or gave an inch. If respect could be measured by weight, I'm pretty sure I gained the proverbial ounce that afternoon.

Then there was Keith Bowman, a 6'6" forward from somewhere on the East Coast. He was twenty-seven or twenty-eight, so I'm fairly certain he was the oldest player on the team at the time. My roommate, Packy Ryan, warned me to be wary of Keith's behavior.

"He's a hothead," Packy proclaimed. On the court, Bowman frightened me. He looked like he was thirty years old, although to eighteen-year-olds, I'm sure most upperclassmen appear more mature. During a pickup game, Bowman objected to my "white on rice" defensive technique.

When players are shut down defensively, they tend to get frustrated. When they're shut down by a freshman.... Well, out of nowhere, this guy started hurling haymaker punches wildly in my direction. But unlike what happened with Wartz, this encounter was polar opposite. Time stood still.

Let me rephrase; everything went to slow-motion mode. He telegraphed every punch, and I simply leaned back and avoided them.

It was like a scene from *Spiderman*. You know, when the bully tries to beat up Peter Parker in the high school hallway, just as he is discovering his newfound superpowers. I felt exactly like Peter Parker. This guy was hurling his best shots, but there was no chance in hell he'd ever be able to connect. "If it continues, this time I'll have to answer with something," I thought. As I plotted my countermeasures, one of the upperclassman yelled at him and snapped him out of his trancelike rage.

Later, he came up to me and apologized. "I'm sorry," he said. "Someone told me you're only eighteen years old. I didn't know."

After that, he did his best to take me under his wing. I certainly didn't want him as my role model, so I avoided him at all cost.

I'd never been exposed to this level of physicality. With few exceptions, my new teammates were simply not the kind of people I cared to associate with. Thankfully, the core group of seniors was the exception to the rule. One in particular was an All-American, Tom Henderson. The 6'4" guard was a member of the 1972 U.S. Olympic basketball team that experienced a heartbreaking loss to the Soviet Union. Though we'd just met, I knew that carrying the humiliation of the basketball nation on his shoulders altered him. The U.S. team never collected its Olympic silver medals, and Henderson returned to the island obsessed with just one thing…winning.

Henderson was a man of few words. He was married and had a young daughter. Tom Henderson was such a consummate professional that whenever I spoke with him, I felt like I was speaking with the head coach. I was rather shy around him, but I could tell he liked me. I like to think he saw my potential. Henderson led the Rainbows to the NIT, then went on to play for the Atlanta Hawks, and later the Washington Bullets and Houston Rockets.

Because of my tenuous relationship with my teammates, I decided Hawaii was not the place for me. I decided to return home. Before I left the island, a prominent booster caught wind of my imminent departure and offered me a car if I would reconsider and stay. Perhaps others saw my potential as well.

I thought my reason for leaving the islands was rock solid. But thirty years later, the true cause would be revealed.

I stood in the middle of my bedroom, weeping uncontrollably. "He fell, he fell," I blurted out through my tears.

My wife rushed to my side. "What are you talking about?" she asked. "Who fell?"

It took me several minutes to answer as I continued to cry. I was experiencing a classic episode of repressed memory syndrome.

The first friend I made in Hawaii was a freshman on the track team. I don't remember his name, but he had sandy blonde hair and was a handsome white guy with a glowing tan. We were both eighteen. He was from the San Francisco Bay area. We became instant best friends and hung out together at every opportunity. One Friday night, he decided to throw a party at his apartment. He wanted to make sure I'd attend. I promised I would. As it happened, though, I met a woman. I figured he wouldn't be disappointed when he learned I'd spent the evening getting laid instead of attending his party.

The following Monday, halfway through practice, a coaching assistant approached me and said, "I'm sorry about your friend." I had no idea what he was talking about and continued to play.

Five minutes later, it dawned on me. I stopped cold in my tracks. A basketball being passed to me hit me in the chest as I lowered my arms and stood frozen. Then I began to weep. I'd heard a freshman had gotten drunk at a party and was playing on the roof of his apartment. He was apparently urinating when he fell to his death.

Out of the blue, I realized why I became deathly afraid of heights during my time in Hawaii. In fact, when I drank, I'd literally crawl to the door of my Hawaii penthouse rather than stand near the railing.

I suffered from post-traumatic stress over the loss of my friend for years and never knew it until the repressed memory came rushing back that day. Then I realized I hadn't left Hawaii because of the questionable character of my teammates. I'd left because I felt responsible for the death of my best friend. If only I'd shown up at the party, he would still be alive, or so I surmised.

You may think I'm being dramatic and wonder how I can call him my best friend when I can't even remember his name. Like many things, I discovered the answer from TV, more precisely from the television series *Kung-Fu*.

Master Kan: Sometimes a stranger known to us for moments can spark our souls to kinships for eternity.

Young Caine: Master, how can strangers take on such importance to our souls?

Master Kan: Because our soul does not record time; it merely records growth.

My soul was injured, and I suppose the only way to heal and carry on was to bury the pain.

CHAPTER 13

LOS ANGELES HARBOR

It was 1974, and I was back home in sunny Southern California with work to do. I'd informed Jim White, basketball coach of Los Angeles Harbor Community College, that I was considering leaving Hawaii, and he immediately offered up a deal.

Harbor College has always had a reputation as kind of a continuation of high school. It was known as a place for students who either didn't have the grades to get into a four-year institution, or couldn't afford to go to one. With enrollment fees a modest ten to thirteen bucks a credit, you can understand why it was an economical choice.

Harbor College is just a stone's throw from the Port of Los Angeles, just off the busy Harbor Freeway, thus the origins of its name. The school's closest neighbor was a Wilmington Oil refinery. It bellowed a toxic aroma that washed across campus, hitching a ride in a fog bank or an ocean breeze.

The school's exterior was unremarkable. Seeing the drab-colored gray brick buildings made me long for the rich colors and lushness of Hawaii. In sharp contrast to the islands, the grass in front of the campus was dry, hard, and always appeared to be on the verge of dying.

Harbor was one of many campuses in the California Community College System that served millions of students with a wide variety of educational and career goals. The California Community College System has always been a breeding ground for a yearly crop of athletic late bloomers and high school superstars whose academic prowess was not up to snuff for four-year institutions. It was basically a farm league for the NCAA.

Harbor College had one thing few other community colleges could boast: its own campus radio station, KHCR. Since my life's dream was to become a disc jockey, the radio station alone was reason enough for me to attend. Before I left Hawaii, my new coach, Jim White, helped me secure an on-air position as a DJ.

My arrival on campus marked the advent of a new era for the Seahawk basketball program. Three of the best ball players in the city were descending on Harbor simultaneously. Grady Roberts was a 6'8" high school All-American who transferred from San Jose State. Eddie Williams was an all-CIF guard who transferred from U.C. Riverside. And then there was me, the 6'10" transfer from the University of Hawaii. Basketball pundits predicted we would have an uncontested dash to the State Championships.

Coach White called in favors from former players and assembled teams from the region's best high schools and colleges to face us. There was Bob Gross from Long Beach State, who went on to star for the Portland Trailblazers and San Diego Clippers, and 6'11" Bill Laimbeer from nearby Palos Verdes High School, who later played for the Cleveland Cavaliers and the Detroit Pistons.

It's hard for me to wrap my head around the fact that Laimbeer went on to be one of the legendary bad boys of the NBA. I thought of him as being a bit of a softy. If memory serves, I did something on the court that made him cry like a baby. Coach White had to console him on the sidelines.

Our Harbor summer league team dismantled all comers, and it increased the buzz about the Seahawks' State Championship prospects. Life was grand for the terrific trio. In fact, I hardly noticed that the rest of the team hated us. It seems Coach White, who had been a father figure to the other players, kicked them to the curb once we arrived. He gave us their summer jobs, which really weren't jobs at all, but more like a wink of an eye.

After we dominated Southern California's other junior colleges with ease, Grady Roberts decided he was too good to play at the junior college level and quit the team. Eddie Williams, on the other hand, had problems academically and fell off the grid after flunking out of school. That left me— and a team that resented me for robbing them of their coach and surrogate father.

Our starting lineup had been set in stone. Coach White told me the offense would revolve around me at center. Eddie would play point guard. Grady would be our power forward, along with Dennis Johnson, a little-known sophomore forward from Dominguez High School. We called Dennis "Red" because he was an African-American boy with freckles and red hair. He was only 6'4", but man, could he jump. I will never forget the first time I played with him. My game was really starting to come around and I could sky. I was going up for a rebound high above the rim. During moments like these, time seems to stand still. My teammate was in a better position to grab the ball, so I let him. At the apex of my jump, I realized this kid was as high as I was. The difference was I was 6'10" and he was a mere 6'4". Dennis Johnson's vertical leap was a half-foot higher than mine. He was the most remarkable jumper I'd ever played against. I mean, he could jump out of the building.

But at the time, Dennis was, how shall I put this delicately? Hmmm. He was nuts. Most of the time, DJ was a steady, quiet guy, but at times, his personality flipped, and he experienced violent emotional outbursts. It was as if he had a dual personality. I don't know whether he had anger issues or some sort of psychosis, but it seemed to me he suffered a double personality syndrome. There was no middle ground with Dennis. When he got angry, for whatever reason (and there didn't need to be a reason), he was dangerous.

One day after practice while leaving the gym, Dennis essentially flipped the switch. To this day, I don't know why he decided to hurl a metal chair at me. There was no indication anything was wrong. I felt the cold air brush my face as the chair came within an inch of my head. He was clearly trying to hurt, if not kill, me. I assumed he was jealous and angry because we had taken their summer jobs, and he had to release his volcano of anger.

In any event, he was dangerous. I said to myself, "Enough! I don't need this." Once again, I walked away from basketball.

The rest of the story is about the unbelievable history of Dennis Johnson. He went on to lead Los Angeles Harbor to the State Championships without Grady, Eddie, or me. But it didn't end there. Dennis Johnson went on to become one of the greatest basketball players in the history of the game. DJ would become a five-time NBA All-Star who wore three NBA championship rings and became a member of the Basketball Hall of Fame.

I saw Dennis many times over the years. Each time, he seemed to have mellowed with age, becoming a stable, mature statesman by the end of his career. When I was a cub sports reporter, he always granted me an interview and anytime access, and I know why. My decision to leave the team put him in a position to succeed. Naturally, there's no doubt he would've started and contributed, but Coach White liked to stick to his game plan. If Grady, Eddie, and I had remained on the team, DJ would not have had the opportunity to become the superstar he was, as the offense was designed around us. Dennis knew this. He never apologized for trying to kill me, but over time, all was forgiven. I grew proud watching his achievements and the fine person he became. Today, I am proud to say DJ was a friend.

> *From the Associated Press:* Dennis Johnson, the star NBA guard who was part of three championships and teamed with Larry Bird on one of the great postseason plays, died Thursday, February 22, 2007, after collapsing at the end of his developmental team's practice. He was 52.

While DJ was slaying the community college system on the basketball court, I was busy making an academic about-face, attending both day and night school, and working as a midday DJ at KHCR. Within a year, I'd garnered more than enough credits to graduate from Harbor with an Associate of Arts degree in Communications.

Coach White, meanwhile, had no idea I'd turned the corner. Why would he? After all, I'd come in with a 0.5 GPA. A few years later, he made a point to call me with a prophetic apology. "I was going through our school records and saw your name on the graduation rolls," he said. "I am so sorry, Paul. I had no idea you graduated," he told me before revealing some upsetting news.

More than 100 colleges had inquired about my availability. Apparently, the University of Southern California, his alma mater, was the most persistent. But, Coach White confessed, he intended to keep me for himself, so he never gave me a single piece of correspondence. His selfish intent was based on his mistaken impression that I was an athlete, not a student.

In retrospect, I found it interesting that I'd received a hundred scholarship offers without stepping foot on the court during the regular season, while DJ, who actually led the team to the California State Championship, received only two.

Despite the hundred inquiries Coach White held back, a few college letters got through. I narrowed the field to Weber State in Utah and Portland State in Oregon, and I accepted invitations to visit both campuses.

CHAPTER 14

PORTLAND STATE

Is it possible for déjà vu to be an understatement? Such was my feeling the first time I saw Portland. It wasn't so much the feeling of having previously experienced something; it was real. Something deep within my soul resonated when I first set eyes on the sleepy river town. As my feet eased off the sidewalk and into the moist, mossy grass on campus, I knew I was home. It was such a soothing, calming experience. I strolled around the campus for hours, speaking to no one, just absorbing the ambience. "Basketball-wise, I'll be a big fish in a small pond here," I thought. More correctly, I was like a salmon returning from the ocean and swimming upstream to return home.

Of course, as you now know, part of my family originated in Oregon. But at the time, I had no knowledge of that. I wouldn't learn about it until I dug through old photos handed down to me when my father died. As I think back now, I wonder whether the spirits of my ancestors were speaking to me that day, celebrating my arrival.

Portland State's coaches showed me a wonderful time on my visit, and they promised the university's basketball program was flowing with resources from boosters. I later found this was far from the truth. In fact, head basketball coach Ken Edwards actually had some players apply for federal poverty assistance in lieu of athletic scholarships.

In my estimation, Coach Edwards had instant credibility. He was a former assistant to Long Beach State coach Jerry Tarkanian. "Tark the Shark" was becoming a coaching legend. The mere association with the Tarkanian name made me think I would be in good hands.

I felt wonderful as I prepared to return to Los Angeles, but not quite comfortable enough to sign the national Letter of Intent to attend PSU. A chance encounter on my way to the terminal changed that. A tall man, dressed in jeans, hiking boots, and a plaid cotton shirt was walking down the concourse. As he drew closer, I noticed his large, unkempt beard. Suddenly, the man zeroed in on me, as if I were lost kin, and began to make a fast approach in my direction. I suddenly realized it was my idol, Bill Walton of the Portland Trailblazers.

"What's happening, brother?" he asked, standing directly in front of me. As I looked up at his shaggy face, he offered his hand. I was flabbergasted. I'd modeled my play after the big redhead, and I considered him one of the greatest basketball players on the planet. Now here he was in the flesh, befriending me.

The deal was done! I would attend Portland State and become best friends with and protégé to the great Bill Walton. Well, as the saying goes, half is better than none at all. The only other time I saw the big redhead in person was following a Blazer shoot-around at Portland Memorial Coliseum when we prepared to face the University of Portland for the city championship.

When I arrived for school in the fall, our coach took me to a nice two-bedroom apartment off Belmont Street in Southeast Portland to meet my new roommate. To my surprise, it was Eddie Williams, the guy who'd vanished from Harbor

College. Eddie was one of the purest shooters I'd ever seen. His form and fingertip release gave him an impressive, picture-perfect jump shot, an absolute thing of beauty. But that beauty would be no match for the beast we would later encounter.

Our apartment was plain and unfurnished. We each received a queen-sized bed and mattress from a secondhand store. We were given a stipend of $250 a month.

That would be the last time we saw our coach until practice. With barely enough money to pay rent, let alone buy meals, we had to fend for ourselves. Eddie supplemented his income by shoplifting food from the local Plaid Pantry. It was a painful fact that I neither condoned nor condemned. On one occasion, I found myself complicit in a crime. Eddie begged me to talk to the store clerk while he was shoplifting. I suppose it was like a child accepting a dare. I didn't want to be perceived as the square from Gardena who "talked like a white boy" and couldn't hang with boys from the hood. But in truth, that's exactly who I was.

In 1975, basketball was not the sport it is today. There was no such thing as a three-point shot, and slam dunks were against the rules. Before the start of the 1967-68 season, the NCAA rules committee banned the dunk from college games. Many people theorized the new rule was instituted to equalize young Lewis Ferdinand Alcindor, the 7'2" center from UCLA who later changed his name to Kareem Abdul-Jabbar. But the rules committee cited numerous injuries as the primary reason for the ban. According to its report, more than 1,500 injuries occurred around the backboard in 1967. Damage to equipment was another factor. Backboards were being shattered and rims bent. In a few cases, games had to be canceled because there was no way to replace the baskets.

PAUL DEAN JACKSON

*"You play one at home, two on the road, and three
if you're losing."*
— From the movie *Glory Road*, referring to the use of
African-American players in college basketball
during the 1960s

On the other hand, long-standing, unspoken rules of the game were abolished.

Reverse discrimination is an issue in sports that has long been swept under the rug. The best man does not always win the starting position. During the '60s, black players had to be twice as good as white players to go half as far. In some sports like football, being twice as good was not good enough. In football, the line of thinking was that blacks did not possess the intellectual capacity to play the quarterback position. In basketball, play-making guards were also thought to be the brains of the outfit, and that position was reserved almost exclusively for white players.

During the early '70s, things became more subtle. Coaches could insert five black players into the game simultaneously if the fans would accept it. While black players began to dominate the field, the deep bench should have displayed a sign that read "Whites Only." Countless backups on NBA benches had received their entry into the league through skin color alone. Fans were hesitant to accept teams with a majority of black players. Once integration was accepted, superior white players became the darlings of the media, taking on superstar status as "The Great White Hope."

When I first learned to play basketball, big men could not handle the rock. That's slang for "dribble the basketball." I was taught that the ball should never touch the ground.

Thanks to players like Edward Ratleff of Long Beach State, that unspoken rule was abolished. I loved it!

It freed me to put the ball on the ground. It gave me a few power strides to wind up for a jumping half-court toss to my new Portland State teammate, whom you could always, and I do mean always, rely upon to be laying in wait, way down yonder.

Let's just say on defense, this free man was a bit of an illusion. A ghost player, a phantom. His entire life depended on having the ball in his personal possession. The court was his. No one else mattered.

I could fly high above the rim and climb upwards to snag a rebound. I'd reel it in, and then ensnare the ball with a hard clap that sent beads of sweat flying. I'd instantly turn to hurl the outlet pass down court. Bam! Two dribbles to elude the defense, and then I'd launch high into the air and blast the basketball over all defenders. By the way, defenders didn't have a chance to stop what was coming because that person you thought was playing defense has long since vanished and is awaiting that pinpoint-accurate pass, giving new meaning to a simple cherry-pick.

Cherry picking, in basketball and certain other sports, refers to play where one player (the cherry picker) does not play defense with the rest of the team, but remains near the opponent's goal. The ball seeks him, like the ring of power seeks its master in *The Lord of the Rings*, for he is the great and powerful Freeman Williams (no relation to Eddie Williams).

I was a great rebounder. I've always had the vision to look down court and the confidence to throw the long pass. That ability whipped the nation's leading scorer into wild frenzies as if he'd orchestrated the entire play from start, right down to the uncontested layup finish. Williams had a flare for the dramatic, and the crowd loved it as he hoisted a single finger in the air after a score as if to say, "I'm number one."

I suppose he would best be described as ruggedly handsome. With his flawless light brown skin, Freeman stood 6'4" in stocking feet and weighed in at a respectable 190 pounds. He wore a full, neatly-trimmed beard close to his face.

Williams was the NCAA Division I men's scoring champion in both the 1977 and '78 seasons. Portland State University's all-time leading scorer was a consensus All-American, whose offensive accomplishments are second only to the legendary "Pistol" Pete Maravich. This is a remarkable feat, considering there was no three-point shot at the time. Simply put, Freeman Williams was a mean, lean, scoring machine.

Now the tell…Freeman's prolific scoring ability was enhanced on more than one occasion by powerful amphetamines like cocaine. Drug use was not so clandestine in the game back then. Everyone on the team, including me, smoked marijuana. But only a few players left the locker room before games and returned with powdered noses and frosty faces. This should not be groundbreaking information to anyone who followed or played college basketball in the '70s. Honestly, Freeman was likely no different from many other players when it came to drug use. The difference was Freeman averaged more than thirty-five points a game.

Perhaps it is petty to disparage the name of a legend. Perhaps it is simply a case of misplaced jealousy or sour grapes. Then again, it could be that Boy Scout talking. You know, the kid who grew up believing in fair play. I suppose you could compare it to the steroid controversy in baseball. Clearly, those who used steroids had an unnatural advantage. Well, I felt the same way about those who used cocaine. It is, after all, a powerful stimulant. It's a non-specific voltage gated sodium channel blocker, which causes it to produce anesthesia-like effects at low doses. In other words, it's also a pain killer.

When I was in high school, my favorite thing about game day was that we were required to wear ties. That tie was our uniform, a symbol of belonging. With ties around our necks, we became official representatives of Gardena High School. Teachers treated us differently. Fellow students gazed at us with respect. Wearing the tie held with it the solemn promise that we would represent our school in the best possible light. It represented good citizenship, sportsmanship, and, most of all, the privilege of being on the high school basketball team.

So I grew up with "No pain, no gain," and I played by the rules. The coaching staff at Portland State University taught me there were no rules. None!

As we taxied away from the gate at the Denver's Stapleton International Airport to return to Portland after a road trip, our jet abruptly stopped just a few yards from the gate, returned to the terminal, and powered down. Security officers boarded our aircraft and ordered us to disembark. We were herded into a back room and told we would have to strip. At this point, two of my teammates stepped up and confessed to their involvement in a diamond heist at the airport gift shop. It was their usual modus operandi. One kept the attendant busy, while the other reached over the counter and stole the goods. In a normal world, they would have been arrested and thrown off the team. At the very least, they would have been suspended from the basketball team. But the world of Portland State basketball was by no means normal. Their punishment? There was none.

One of those same players physically assaulted our coach in the locker room after a home game. I stood in absolute shock, unable to move, after he punched the coach relentlessly. Ken Edwards made a hasty retreat from the locker room, but not before being the recipient of a swift kick in the ass by his attacker before security took him away. His punishment? There was none.

Another player attempted to choke a referee after a game against the University of Puget Sound. During the game, fans used the N-word to taunt members of our team. This player, by the way, was also involved in the infamous Denver diamond heist. The punishment? Well, you should get the picture by now. There was none.

It was a profound lesson: if you are good enough in basketball, you are free to do as you please.

How could I hold true to the values of truth or consequences instilled in me over a lifetime? Calling me disillusioned would be an understatement.

These are just a few of the unconscionable capers performed by members of the Portland State basketball squad. I say in all honesty that on virtually every road trip, one of my teammates committed a serious crime.

With the exception of a couple of players, I was living with criminals. I was the odd man out. As the honest outcast, I spent my life living by the Boy Scout creed. Unfortunately, being trustworthy, loyal, helpful, friendly, courteous, kind, obedient, cheerful, thrifty, brave, clean, and reverent with this group was like wearing a sign on my back that said, "Kick Me."

One day, I left the PSU gym with my head down and shoulders slumped. This clearly demonstrated the body language of a boy who had gone a long day because no one had told him about the "Kick Me" sign on his back.

Then, I heard a friendly voice cry out, "How's it going, big guy?"

A small man with a big voice greeted me as if he knew I was down. It was PSU head football coach Darrel "Mouse" Davis. I thought no one noticed the criminality of my teammates. Davis, however, had been quietly observing the exploits of the basketball team and, apparently, sensed that I needed a friend.

When I turned to face him, it occurred to me that never once had my own basketball coach asked how I was doing. It was the first time I had a productive conversation with someone from the athletic department.

Davis was a ball of energy. He got the nickname "Mouse" because of his physical stature. He stood 5'4" on a good day…a very good day. His optimistic manner and presence lifted my spirits. He inquired about my wellbeing and asked how I was enjoying the city. It was enough to know that someone was watching and respected me.

It seemed that wherever I went, athletics were evolving, making history. As it so happened, Darrel "Mouse" Davis was busy changing the face of NCAA football by implementing a "run and shoot" offense in the college game. This new style of football utilized just one running back, with up to four wide receivers. The receivers were charged with making on-the-fly adjustments to different defensive schemes. With that many receivers in the mix, the passing option was usually available, and Viking football was reborn…airborne.

Davis had a quarterback named June Jones, whom, coincidently, was the starting quarterback at the University of Hawaii during my freshman year there. Like me, Jones had played for three colleges: Oregon, Hawaii, and finally, Portland State. There, he brought legitimacy to the run and shoot, racking up 5,798 yards passing, with fifty touchdowns over his two seasons. Jones played for the Atlanta Falcons for three years and spent time in the Canadian football league. After his pro career, he became Mouse Davis' protégé, and then went on to become a successful college coach at the University of Hawaii and Southern Methodist University.

Mouse Davis was a harbinger of hope for me. After our first encounter, he made it a point to chat with me. I, in return, watched with joy as my new friend constructed the most entertaining football program in the land. After Jones graduated, All-American quarterback Neil Lomax stepped up to the line. While Freeman Williams was making headlines as the nation's leading scorer in basketball, Neil Lomax and wide receiver Clint Didier were setting scoring records in football. The team scored a 105-0 victory against a hapless Delaware State. That same Vikings team also went on to set an NCAA 1-AA record of ninety-three points against Cal Poly Pomona. Lomax and Didier had long and fruitful professional careers, in part due to the tutelage of Mouse Davis, the one man at Portland State who saw me for who I was: a good kid in a bad situation.

I don't know when or why I lost the respect of my coach. Perhaps I never had it. I do know when I lost the respect of my teammates, and it had nothing to do with their thievery. It happened during a game against Colorado State University.

Let's back up a bit. When I chose my college courses, I tried to make my life as easy as possible. I always chose at least one "easy" credit. One day, I checked the schedule of classes and decided to take beginning karate. The class, which was held in the PSU athletic complex, turned out to be quite enjoyable. We learned basic moves. There was some punching, but it was mostly defensive techniques.

A week before a road trip to Colorado, we learned how to defend against a basic chokehold. For a week, we practiced a quick and easy way to remove an attacker's hands from around our throats. Once we learned how to escape a chokehold, we were taught a follow-up move, a retaliation blow. Our instructor warned that such a vicious blow could potentially result in severe injury, or even death. It was possible, he explained, to push the attacker's nose into his skull. We practiced this move dozens of times.

Later, in our game against Colorado State, a fight broke out on the court between players. As I turned to see what was happening, the center from Colorado State suddenly reached out, grabbed me around my neck, and began to choke me. He was 6'8" and one of the only players I'd ever encountered who was skinnier than I was. I looked into his eyes and realized he was frightened. I was surprised, rather than in any sort of pain or distress, because his hand seemed weak. I looked at him for a moment in disbelief, and then I proceeded to remove his hands from my neck as I had been taught. The move worked perfectly! His arms went high into the air, and a look of terror washed over his face as I rendered him defenseless. He looked up helplessly, and his eyes pleaded with me not to hurt him. I'd never felt more in control of a situation at any other time in my life. I contemplated my follow-through, but all I could see was a skinny kid who looked frightened out of his mind. It was up to me. I could come down hard on the bridge of his nose, and hospitalize him or worse. At that moment, I decided I could not maim him. I achieved my goal by quickly removing his hands from my body. As he stared at me, I waited a moment to see whether he might lash out again. If he did, I would be obliged to destroy him. When he did not, I looked him in the eye again, shook my head in disgust, and then simply walked to the bench.

My teammates never let me hear the end of it. They didn't know that I'd spent the week working on a move that could kill a man in that very situation. And I never told them. Heck, even if I'd told them, they wouldn't have believed me. All they saw was that I was being choked.

"You let that guy choke you," Freeman Williams joyfully reminded me. And he never let me forget it.

I'd been competing for the starting center position against a blonde-haired, blue-eyed 6'8" junior transfer from Portland Community College. Mike Richardson was a lumbering, Nordic-looking dude, so it seemed fitting he should be a Viking. After all, it was PSU's mascot. Mike was five years older than I was. He was married, had a home in the area, and even owned a car! It was a sporty Opel GT, a major bonus. Mike was an extraordinary artist. He often shared his paintings which was rich in character and color.

If you ask me, we were two players of equal talent. One was a bit more mobile, could jump a little higher, and was a tad quicker and a little better on defense. That's my assessment of me. The other player was reliable on the boards, able to fill big holes in the middle on defense, and a tad better on offense. That's my assessment of Mike.

Mike remembers his assessment of me:

> As far as our skills, you have your perception, and I have mine. I believe I played better in practice leading up to the season. I think I was a better

defender and equal rebounder. I was definitely a
better passer. I also set a lot of screens for Freeman so
he could shoot. I don't think that was something you
ever considered. I had three or four really good
games.

I think you were probably a better offensive player.
As far as "lumbering," that's funny because I thought
the same about you. But maybe it was true about me.
I was having issues with my knee, and that could have
affected me, but previously, my game had flourished
precisely because of the way I ran the floor.

Other than Mike, the starters on our team were black. So,
judging from the history of discrimination in basketball I
presented earlier, who do you think got more playing time in
Portland, Oregon? Yes, I called the race card, but there was a
little more involved.

After the choking incident in Colorado, Mike's stock went
through the roof.

Mike and I roomed together on road trips, and I enjoyed his
company. He loves to recall our many adventures together,
especially a game against the Air Force Academy. The
general's daughter took a shine to me, and we all spent the
evening partying in a nuclear missile silo.

We were both astonished by the reckless abandon with
which our coaches consumed alcohol, particularly vodka, on
road trips. If we needed to seek them out for any reason,
we'd find Ken Edwards red-faced, getting hammered with an
assistant coach.

Our coaches led by example, and we *all* followed. I thought
nothing of drinking on the road. When you're young and

powerful, you have no idea how much energy can be depleted from your body after an evening of heavy drinking.

An All-American training table would've helped us all. But that was not happening during the Ken Edward era at Portland State University. While traveling, the meal money was allotted to Freeman. He handed it out to teammates as he pleased, and though he never shorted me, getting my money was like pulling teeth. It was humiliating.

CHAPTER 15

TRAIL'S END

In Oregon, fall is an amazing time. Nature paints the region in extraordinary colors that comfort the soul. The kiss of chilly damp air washing across the face invigorates, especially while walking. And so it was that my mood was bright, my pace quick, as every step brought me closer to home...the campus of Portland State University, located in a beautiful section of the city called the Park Blocks. A continuous stand of American elms and big-leaf maples line the street, creating a tranquil corridor of colorful shade trees in the summer months.

I'd breezed through this section of the city hundreds of times, but on this particular night, the sound of bubbling fountains brought my attention to the statues. Bronze men stood as sentries, as if to ensure the serenity of the moment. I paused to listen, and then proceeded across the invisible line that dichotomizes the city from the University campus.

As I reached the end of my saunter, near the southern edge of campus, the quiet was broken by the faint roar of a distant crowd. As I moved toward the source, my heart sank and I began to feel a profound sense of loss and sadness I had never known before. As the crowd noise grew louder, my melancholy increased correspondingly.

Like Superman walking toward kryptonite, each step I took seemed to annihilate part of my life energy. My legs became heavy, but I pushed on until I could no longer move. Paralyzed by a crippling depression, I found myself standing completely alone outside the PSU athletic complex, listening to the crowd react to the basketball game inside. Releasing a deep sigh, I thought about walking in. But I couldn't move. Pride would not let me.

To this day, I am not sure how long I stood at trail's end in the park, staring at the PSU sports complex like a coyote that had been chased away from a prime meal by a pack of wolves. Thinking back, that analogy might not be far from the truth. A few days earlier, I'd made the most important decision of my young life. Now I was questioning myself.

"Doubt is a pain too lonely to know that faith
is his twin brother."

— Khalil Gibran

The last game I ever played for Portland State University was the first game of the 1978 season. I'd spent the summer running Southern California beaches, doing push-ups, sit-ups, and playing basketball every day. I was at the top of my game and was determined to show the world what I was made of. From the first day of practice, I finished first in every drill. The suicide drills that had so depleted me in earlier years were nothing. I was running on air.

I was fairly sure I'd start that first game, even though Coach Edwards had not announced his starting lineup.

I did not start. Sitting there, I took in the scene. I was sure I would dominate when I went in. When the first half ended and I hadn't played, I was devastated. Fully expecting to start in the second half, I again sat the pine. When I looked up at the coaches from the end of the bench, I could see Ken

Edwards was stammering drunk. I wondered whether he even knew I was on the bench.

Apparently, he just couldn't handle the pressure of the game, so he must've had a few belts during halftime in addition to what he'd ingested before the game. I think in the end, it really didn't matter whether we won or lost, as long as Freeman got his points and the crowd got its show. Utterly humiliated, after the game I quietly packed my bags, turned in my uniform, and never returned to basketball.

I hold Portland State partly responsible for the downfall of countless African-American athletes during the 1970s. A mere statistical review of graduation rates among the basketball team would have yielded an astounding truth. The University used players for their athletic prowess alone. Not only were they allowed to run amuck outside the law, but they weren't even required to attend class. When I returned to campus that fall in 1978, I was shocked to learn that every member of the basketball team had been awarded six summer credits from Cal State Los Angeles to ensure our athletic eligibility. Needless to say, I never attended CSULA, nor did I need the credits to remain eligible.

The true menace was Head Coach Ken Edwards, who knowingly allowed criminal behavior from his players and took part in such activity himself, as evidenced by what later became known as the PSU credit scandal. An industrious reporter from KOIN-TV Portland broke the story after soliciting my college transcripts as evidence.

Clearly, PSU administrators did not care about what happened in the classroom, as long as we could play hoops. And while the majority of the players of that era were good at stealing the ball, a minority was even better at stealing food, alcohol, and various trinkets. In the end, their larceny did not go unpunished. They were robbed of their futures. Chasing the dream of stardom, they were robbed of an education. And when the best of them, Freeman Williams, finally achieved the NBA dream as a first round draft pick, he was ill-equipped to handle it. Drafted by Boston, Williams was dealt to the Clippers, where he had a good run, but his career was cut short, allegedly by drug abuse. Williams has admittedly fought drug addiction, squandering his NBA earnings like countless players before him.

Mike Richardson continued with art, and eventually, he opened a small comic book store called Dark Horse. He grew his little shop into a successful movie production company. He confided in me his plans to one day make a movie about Freeman and our experiences at Portland State. Here's the thing about Mike: while we reminisced about the dirty deeds committed by our teammates, he said, "I just couldn't understand you."

Sadly, I knew exactly what he meant. I'd heard it before. It is difficult for some people to understand a black man with no stereotypical dialect. No slang, no gangs, no bullshit. I broke that mold. What you see is what you get, and I suppose a first experience with an upper-middle class black kid from the South Bay of Los Angeles was beyond the realm of understanding for a white guy from Oregon. It was clear that despite all his artistry and mastery of colors, Mike still saw some things, especially people, in black and white.

After completing the paragraph above, I decided to reach out to my old friend to address the elephant in the room at last. Subsequently, Richardson responded:

> In the end, it's insulting and kind of sad. I always liked you. I thought you were a smart guy (well, maybe not in your early choice of women). I could not care less about

what you or anyone thinks of me as a basketball player, but to see me as someone who looks at people through a race prism is disappointing. I will say again, I never thought a single thing about your articulation or your background. I grew up in Italian farm country. Even as a youngster, race was never an issue with me. I wasn't even aware of it. You should know that from our adventures together. As a kid, my heroes were Bill Russell and Muhammad Ali. Never once did the color of their skin or the classic stereotypes you refer to ever color my own thinking.

I congratulate my old friend for being the only person I've ever known in this great nation of ours who does not see color. I say this in jest, as Mike loves to remember "being the only white guy on a team of black players."

I am sure he will produce another box office smash about that very topic. You cannot live through the times we did and not see race. In my opinion, anyone who makes such a fantastic claim about race is either a saint or insane. I like to think that those of us who see and experience the richness of diversity dwell in the place between.

Mike stepped up to the plate in an attempt to help Freeman Williams get his diploma. "I brought him up to Portland and helped him get established. Freeman was always a gentleman. He attended my daughter's basketball games. He replaced his drug habit with a sweet tooth."

I believe PSU should honor its past athletes by allowing all non-graduates of that era the opportunity to reenter college (at no cost) in a real attempt to attain an actual degree. After all, it's never too late to learn.

So now, when you see the great Freeman Williams' name directly under the legendary Pistol Pete Maravich's name as the second all-time leading scorer in NCAA history, I think an asterisk is in order.

Eventually, I was able to move forward and not look back. After leaving basketball, I was once again able to double my efforts in the classroom. I graduated from Portland State with a B.S. in speech communications, with an emphasis on intercultural communications.

Mike and I are members of an exclusive club, scholarship basketball players who actually received a degree from Portland State University. Tragically, there are not enough former basketball graduates from that era to make up a five-man team.

In a strange twist of fate, history would repeat itself in terms of basketball for me. The sport was far from out of my system, so I decided to try out for the Portland Trailblazers. I called the Blazers' front office. To my great surprise, they said they'd be happy to have me attend rookie camp. I'd stayed in shape, playing basketball every day. But on the day the camp was to begin, I hadn't heard a peep from the Blazers. Frustrated, I decided to call the front office again.

"Paul, we've been looking for you," a Blazer representative told me over the phone. "We left several messages with the athletic department, asking them to please relay our message to you."

It stung of Jim White's admission that he'd withheld college recruiting letters from me because he thought I had not graduated from Harbor College. But this was something different. I assume messages from the Trailblazers went to the basketball office and were discarded immediately. The office staff certainly knew where to find me since I worked out in the gym every day.

Not missing a beat, I grabbed my tennis shoes and rode to Portland Memorial Coliseum with my girlfriend, Tina, who borrowed a car from her uncle. I made it just in time for the afternoon workout.

It was an honor just to be on the floor, as the Blazers considered this class to be the best rookie camp in the team's history. It consisted of Michael Thompson (first-round draft pick, who was not required to attend), Clemon Johnson, Ron Brewer, Keith Herron. All of them, along with a host of other NCAA notables, had prolific NBA careers.

I was impressive during rookie camp. I held my own against all comers, and Trailblazer head coach Dr. Jack Ramsey took notice. As I mentioned earlier, Trailblazers superstar Bill Walton was my idol. I modeled my play after his, and apparently, it showed. By the second day, it seemed I might have a chance at staying on the team beyond the first cut. Coach Ramsey called me by name and seemed to be appreciative of my play.

Then it happened. I came down wrong after grabbing a rebound. I rolled my ankle, and the swelling began. I suppose I probably should've told the trainer, but at the time, Bill Walton was sidelined with a foot injury, and I figured the last thing the Blazers wanted to hear about was another big man with an injured foot. I kept the injury private and was only able to continue at three-quarter speed. Coach Ramsey moved on, and I was cut after the rookie game. I did manage to grab several rebounds and even scored two points. A perfectly-timed slam dunk, over a crowd of players. The move brought thundering applause from the fans for the skinny kid from Portland State.

That single play sent a clear message that PSU missed out the moment I quit the team. That thought has sustained me to this day.

Over the course of my summers in Los Angeles, I became friends with Bob Jones, a basketball scout from the South Bay. Jones looked like a sun-washed surfer dude, but he had just one love: basketball. He arranged pick-up games between the best players in South Bay Los Angeles, chauffeuring me and Gig Sims (who went on to play for UCLA) to various venues in his beat-up convertible VW Bug.

On one occasion, he invited me to accompany him to a UCLA basketball game. At the conclusion, he said he needed to make a quick stop before taking me home. We ended up cruising to Brentwood to visit Kiki Vandeweghe. Until then, I'd only seen Kiki when we played pick-up games over the summer in UCLA's Poly Pavilion. I admired every aspect of his game, and I was a little envious because he was always the first player chosen if a team needed an extra man for a pick-up game. That slot was normally reserved for me, if Vandeweghe was not around, because everyone knew I could rebound and was more than happy to play defense. I watched Kiki closely; he never seemed to struggle while playing. He just quietly dominated.

I had no idea Kiki was rich. It was my first visit to a mansion. I sat quietly, taking it in, as Bob chatted with Kiki's father, Dr. Earnest Vandeweghe, a noted pediatrician. Did I mention that Dr. Vandeweghe also happened to be a standout player for the New York Nicks in the '50s? Kiki's mom, a former Miss America, offered me a cool drink. I sipped my soda and took in the opulence. I wondered why someone with so much would bother to accept an athletic scholarship, but I knew exactly why it should be offered.

Kiki Vandeweghe was a class act. I was impressed with his laid-back demeanor. When he was on the court, the brothers were on their best behavior. Dirty fouls, trash talking, and, most of all, fighting were not acceptable when he was on the court. That's one reason I loved to play pick-up games in Poly. Kiki had a long and successful career in the pros, and he went on to become general manager of the Denver Nuggets.

Following my tryout with the Portland Trailblazers, Bob contacted me and said he'd secured a contract for me to play in Europe. It would pay ten-thousand dollars, he told me. "Ten-thousand dollars is free and clear money for you to take home. Everything else is paid for," he assured me.

Something about the deal just didn't seem right. I assumed Bob would pocket the lion's share of whatever the true value of the contract might be. And so I turned down an opportunity to play professional basketball in Europe.

CHAPTER 16

ALL WORK AND NO PLAY

In my first job out of college, I worked for United Grocers in a Portland suburb. UG had the distinction of being the highest-paying warehouse in the United States. I worked the overnight shift, filling orders for various grocery chains. I drove a small tractor called a "Barrett," with a flatbed in tow, around a huge warehouse, collecting every type of food. The heaviest items first, and potato chips on top. The items were stacked on wooden pallets. My pallets were generally asymmetrical and always a little off balance as I was still mastering the art of being a Barrett operator. When the store's order was complete, I pulled my cart to a central track that ran through the center of the warehouse. From there, the goods circled the warehouse until a forklift driver snagged them and loaded them in waiting trucks.

It was a fast-paced environment, filled with danger. Since the jobs paid so well, everyone hustled. Early on, I was attaching a cart to the track when it failed to attach. The procession of carts, of course, pushed my cart along, and my leg got trapped. I stood erect and watched helplessly because I knew what was next. The rear cart pushed the front cart in a scissor motion with my leg in the middle. I closed my eyes and waited for my leg to be crushed or severed. The moment the cart touched my pants, the conveyor stopped. As I looked up, one of the veteran warehousemen had pushed the emergency stop. I have no doubt he saved me from losing my leg.

Soon after, while passing a dividing door of the warehouse on my Barrett, a forklift driver accelerated over the central track to try to beat some carts. It was much like a railroad crossing. The forklift driver's intent was to speed through to the other side of the warehouse before the train arrived. I saw him out of the corner of my eye and figured out what he was about to do. I hopped off my Barrett a second before he nailed it to the side wall. Had I not disembarked, I would've been impaled. I'd managed to escape death or serious injury once again. At that point, I decided I should search for a new job.

CHAPTER 17

THE KYTE

A nd so I decided to pursue my lifelong dream. It had been, and will always be, my desire to be a disc jockey. Truly, the first words I absorbed as a child were, "Burn, baby, burn," a sly reference to hot records created by a '60s DJ who called himself the Magnificent Montague.

KGFJ was Southern California's soul music station. When we were in the car, my older sister twisted the AM dial to the 1200 mark, and then she wiggled it back and forth until we heard the amazing voices of people like us on the radio. Black people.

Every hour, the station aired local news with Larry McCormick. The DJs tossed to him, and it was all business. And he pulled it off with not so much as a slight stutter or mispronounced word. His voice was clear, assuring, and professional. I knew nothing of news, and likely understood only a few of the news stories, but when Larry McCormick was on the air, I felt proud to be black. He clearly knew what he was doing, I thought. No jive talking, but a black man in control, telling us about the events that were unfolding around us. Little did I know our lives would intersect one day.

After applying at dozens of Portland radio stations, it took only a couple of weeks before I was hired by KYTE AM and FM as the station page. For the next few months, I made the morning coffee, relieved the receptionist at the front desk when she needed a break, and dependably ran any and all errands asked of me.

KYTE was a new acquisition of the Gaylord Broadcasting Company, a growing Texas-based media conglomerate that was busy swallowing up media outlets around the nation. Gaylord purchased KYTE from KOIN-TV, the CBS television affiliate station in Portland. It immediately changed call signs from KOIN radio to KYTE (Kite) and set about building a new state-of-the-art studio to house its new AM and FM combo stations, just off Front Street, on the banks of the Willamette River.

When I joined the station, it was still broadcasting from the KOIN-TV building. Every morning, I went to the TV station to collect the mail. I found it exciting to see the TV personalities I'd enjoyed watching from time to time in college.

It was there I met KYTE's morning DJ, a huge man named Gordon Scott. He stood 6' 4" and may have weighed close to 400 pounds. This mountain of a man was everyone's adorable teddy bear. It seemed every few minutes someone would walk by and pop in to wish him a good morning, and each time I visited, I realized why. Each day, I peered into the studio and said good morning. One day, he invited me in, and when I tried to leave, he said, "Stay here! Tell them I told you to stay here. You need to learn how to do this." He pointed to the control board in front of him. When he flipped the switch and the on-air light outside the studio door illuminated, magic happened. His voice was friendly, full of life, informative, and conversational. I absorbed every word. I studied his mouth in its position to the microphone. I watched his hands as they sat on the studio board, ready to fire the next event.

"You're listing to KYTE Portland," he would say, then quickly pot the mic down with one hand and artfully start a song with the other. In those days, songs were placed on carts. They resembled eight-track tapes in appearance. They went the way of the dinosaur in 1982 and were replaced by standard cassette tapes. Radio carts were used to record virtually everything that went on-air, from commercials to music. Each cart was encoded with an electronic signal that flashed a light in the studio so the DJ would know the song was ending.

Almost daily, as I was caught up in the magic of watching Gordon, the phone would ring in the studio. "Where is Paul?" a voice would say. "We need the mail."

Gordon would reply indignantly, "He's with me in the studio, and he's learning."

President John F. Kennedy introduced the term affirmative action in 1961 as a method of remedying discrimination. In 1978, it was being attacked as reverse discrimination in some quarters. Thankfully, not at KYTE Radio Portland, which had adopted a country music format. Besides me, Japanese production assistant Steve Naganuma was the only other person of color on staff. When the higher-ups from Gaylord Broadcasting came to town, they seemed to take a special interest in me when I was answering telephones at the front desk. I must have been quite an oddity to them. I was a tall, skinny black kid, with a big afro and scraggly beard, who was polite, respectful, and articulate. I'm certain they instructed our station manager to move me up the food chain for the sake of affirmative action. And so, when the new studio was finally completed, I was promoted to the position of automation engineer.

The job required a third-class broadcast license from the Federal Communications Commission. The license was required to reduce the station's operating power after sunset. We referred to the power change as going directional because directional antennas were used at night in order to protect other radio stations' signals, or sky wave services. Otherwise, we'd be broadcasting well into Canada because the way AM signals travel in the ionosphere changes dramatically from daytime to nighttime. It's a highfalutin' way of saying that I had to flip a switch and sign the log to confirm we'd made the power change. I spent the rest of my shift babysitting a massive robot, referred to as FM automation. Even during radio's heydays, broadcast companies were looking for ways to reduce cost. Automation was the way of the future. It eliminated an entire overnight shift, as the robot could do everything as well as a DJ, with the exception of actually talking.

Afternoon announcers prerecorded one liners, and automation took it from there. It required nightly feedings of carts (tapes) into the on-air rotations. Each cart had a sensor as well as a coded queue that flashed an external light to indicate one song was ending, and another event was about to occur. It was quite a sight; the maniacal gismo filled an entire back room of the station.

What a gig. I sipped coffee to stay awake. I made sure the robot was on the job, with no glitches that would produce dead air. In radio, dead air is the ultimate sin. The term refers to dead silence on the radio.

When I got bored watching "HAL," I amused myself with a trick I learned from my compadre Wayne Anderson, a fellow automation engineer. Wayne is a story in and of himself. If you saw the movie *Wayne's World* and saw Wayne

Anderson, you might get the feeling that someone made a movie about his life and didn't tell him.

The trick Wayne taught me was to pull automation carts out of the machine and replace them with others. It was simple things, like replacing Smoky and the Bandit's "East Bound and Down" to "West Bound and Down" to see whether anyone noticed. To my knowledge, no one did. It was a secret way to play DJ.

The automation system was quite reliable, so after the night staff departed, I usually disappeared into the station's plush production studio and cut my own party mix of studio-quality cassette tapes. My taste was eclectic, and I could choose anything I wished from the station's massive music library.

You may wonder, "What kind of conscientious automation engineer leaves his job in the middle of the shift?" Well, I piped the station's audio into the studio to ensure there was no dead air. Better yet, I had permission…from the Voice of God.

There's an old term only old-school broadcasters would understand: "Voice of God." I understood the phrase the moment I heard Bob Brooks recite the station's call letters, "KYTE, Portland." It was a ballsy voice, just enough bass, mixed with sheer brilliance.

Bob was our production director. His voice was the station's signature. His was the most recognized voice in the Pacific Northwest. His commercials ran from the California border right up to the Canadian line. Bob was stout, had a large chest, and a brown sun-washed, leathery face. I thought him to be the most interesting man in the world. He was a Vietnam veteran, so I inquired, "Did you see any action?" or something to that effect.

His expression carried the hardness of a man who'd seen the worst kind of it.

I never brought up the topic again. The blotches on his skin, I surmised, must be from spending too much time in the jungle in fields of Agent Orange.

Bob was a chain smoker, and a man who liked to drink. I felt like he could handle himself in just about any circumstance. And for reasons unknown to me, I'm honored to say he let me hang with him, and he introduced me to his crew, including Kurt Matthews, a TV anchor at KOIN. Man, Kurt was a whirlwind. He fell in love with his co-anchor, left his wife, and then flew off to follow his new girlfriend to Hawaii. I was enthralled, to say the least. Then there was Ed Whelan, another of Bob's closest confidants. Ed was the weekend sports anchor at KOIN TV. He was also one of only three blacks on TV in Portland at the time. When Bob and his crew's shifts ended at 11:30, we prowled the streets of Portland or spent late nights drinking heavily at a local bar named the Veritable Quandary.

I was in the hands of mentors who took care of me—right down to finding the right woman. Bob and Gordon thought I should ask out a lovely new reporter at KOIN TV. She'd been hired from a television station in Spokane. I suppose they thought we'd be a good match because she wasn't white nor black; she was truly multicultural. Her father was part Native American, French, German, and Scottish, and her mother was from Japan.

I thought she was drop-dead gorgeous, and so, on their advice, I pursued her. I think she was surprised the first time I asked her out. But she politely declined. I assumed it was because she was a general assignment reporter and I was a gofer. But after our first encounter, I found her to be nice, polite, somewhat soft-spoken, and professional. I was bewitched and thought I'd take another shot at it.

Since I still had access to the television station, I could just happen to run into her in the hallway—which I did. She responded with a smile. One more try was all it took. Message received loud and clear, she simply was not interested.

So why do I mention this quick one-sided flirtation with Ann Curry? Well, she's attractive, and she's famous. But the bigger point is that my mentors had extraordinary class and taste. After all, Gordon Scott and Bob Brooks were extraordinary gentlemen.

Bob took me under his wing. He taught me almost every aspect of radio production, beginning with recording a vinyl record to a cart, an interesting process that involved operating a turntable with one hand and the cart machine with the other. The record had to be a precise half-counterrevolution from the song's intro. Bob explained this had to be done precisely, and I could never vary this procedure; otherwise, the song's intro would not be up to speed.

Growing up in a world that I think sometimes devalues African-American men, I couldn't help but feel that Gordon and Bob embraced and uplifted me because I was black. Both were truly evolved, and though they never spoke to me about race, you knew they were the kind of men who would never allow racism. I was just another person to them. I felt blessed to be in the good graces of these two men, who were giants in the industry in the Pacific Northwest.

Bob assembled, and then empowered, the station's "oddballs." He staged a quiet revolution and made Steve Naganuma his production assistant. This put an Asian male on the air in Portland for the first time. He mentored me, and, at the request of an insistent member of sales, allowed me to voice my first radio commercials, a thirty-second spot for a new R&B group called Maze, and another for an old group named the Jacksons.

He showed me how to splice tape. In the '80s, we recorded on tape. If there was an untimely gap, we needed to splice (cut) the tape with a razorblade in the spot we wanted to make the desired change. Then we taped it back together.

He was careful to teach me about audio levels, and how never to over-modulate. Soon I became a scientist of sound, creating and announcing my own private mixes. I produced wild promos for J.W. Friday at KBOO, a public access station. J.W. had the only R&B show in town.

I made a special tape for my first ride, a 1970 Volkswagen bus. I titled it "Van on the Run." It usually took my passengers several minutes to realize it was a tape and not the radio. After I announced Paul McCartney with "Van on the Run," everyone usually got a kick out of it.

CHAPTER 18

SHAME ON THE MOON

Free albums were a regular benefit of working for a radio station. Many were pre-release copies and some never made it on air. One day, I grabbed a pre-release from the artist Rodney Crowell to look at the cover. Bob told me Crowell was a talented young musician who wrote for Tanya Tucker. On his advice, I took the album home and gave it a listen. Simple guitar chords, accompanied by bluesy piano flourishes, float through the cautionary lyrics.

Shame on the Moon©

Till you've been beside a man
You don't know what he wants
You don't know if he cries at night
You don't know if he don't

When nothin' comes easy
Old nightmares are real
Until you've been beside a man
You don't know how he feels

Once inside a woman's heart
A man must keep his head
And heaven opens up the door
Where angels fear to tread

PAUL DEAN JACKSON

Some men go crazy
Some men go slow
And some men go just where they want
And some men never go.

Oh, blame it on midnight
Ooh, shame on the moon

Everywhere it's all around
Comfort in a crowd
Strangers faces all about
Laughin' right out loud

Hey, watch where you're goin'
Step light on your toes
Until you've been beside a man
You don't know who he knows

Oh, blame it on midnight
Ooh, shame on the moon

Oh, blame it on midnight
Ooh, shame on the moon

Those lyrics seemed to speak to my life. "Shame on the Moon" has echoed in my mind through many chapters of my life. Through the good times, as well as when my world seemed a bit off kilter. In my case, the world was my body, mind, and soul. The song made perfect sense to me.

Why "Shame on the Moon"? you might ask. Well, science teaches us that the moon keeps the earth in perfect balance. Of all the billions of objects in the galaxy we call the Milky Way, only the moon affects the core of the earth. And what does that core exist of? Mostly water. Water covers 71 percent of the world, and it also exists in the realm of the unseen as vapor.

Our bodies are more than 60 percent water; blood is 92 percent water. Our brains, which float our consciousness, sail on an ocean that is 75 percent water. In my opinion, the moon's gravitational pull on the very core of our being can be likened to a thread that pushes and pulls not only the oceans of Mother Earth, but also the vast depths of the oceans of our minds. Therefore, the moon's gravitational pull must strongly impact us—body, mind, and soul.

Creedence Clearwater Revival released a song about the moon's gravitational pull on us in the 1969 song "Bad Moon Rising[©]," written by John Fogarty.

I see a bad moon rising.
I see trouble on the way.
I see earthquakes and lightnin'.
I see bad times today.

Don't go around tonight,
Well it's bound to take your life,
There's a bad moon on the rise.

I hear hurricanes a-blowing.
I know the end is coming soon.
I fear rivers over-flowing.
I hear the voice of rage and ruin.

Well don't go around tonight,
Well it's bound to take your life,
There's a bad moon on the rise.

Hope you got your things together.
Hope you are quite prepared to die.
Looks like we're in for nasty weather.
One eye is taken for an eye.

PAUL DEAN JACKSON

Well don't go around tonight,
Well it's bound to take your life,
There's a bad moon on the rise.

Don't come around tonight,
Well it's bound to take your life,
There's a bad moon on the rise

John Fogarty saw the gravitational pull of what I assume was a full moon as a negative effect on our consciousness. But as I have come to understand, we cannot fault the moon for perceived negatives on the planet.

In his haunting lyrics, Rodney Crowell blames time. He does not hold time in general responsible, but instead blames midnight, specifically. Midnight, the proverbial witching hour, believed to be the moment when ghosts and demons appear. Those are our inner demons, which are generally associated with a time of bad luck. Midnight, however, is also the moment of transition from one day to the next.

"Having spent the better part of my life trying to either relive the past or experience the future before it arrives, I have come to believe that in between these two extremes is peace."

— Author Unknown

Or as Harriet Beecher Stowe so aptly stated, "The past, the present, and the future are really one: they are today."

"Shame on the Moon" became my gospel. It taught me not to make assumptions about people, not to judge.

Till you've been beside a man
You don't know what he wants
You don't know if he cries at night
You don't know if he don't

It also taught me caution is advised in a world that can sometimes be wrought with hidden dangers.

Hey, watch where you're goin'
Step light on your toes
Until you've been beside a man
You don't know who he knows

I prefer to change the last stanza (when I sing the song to myself) and replace the word "who" with "what."

Until you've been beside a man
You don't know *what* he knows.
Oh, blame it on midnight
Ooh, shame on the moon.

Being tall brings unavoidable notoriety. If you happen to be tall and black, that stature brings with it an inescapable stereotype. I call it the "Do you play basketball?" equation. If the answer is no, then most people (at least the thousands I've encountered) deem it an utter waste of human potential. If you happen to be in the 98th percentile in height as I am (less than 2 percent of the world's population is taller), the equation is no longer, "Do you play basketball?" The question is an emphatic, "Who do you play for?"

In a world that celebrates large men with a ball in hand, folks wrench in disbelief to learn I am not a professional basketball player. "Why not?" they cry. "What a waste!"

I, meanwhile, quietly recite, "Blame it on midnight. Shame on the moon."

I found it interesting that some years later, Bob Segar and the Silver Bullet Band remade "Shame on the Moon," and it became a mega hit on *The Distant* album. Suddenly, my gospel according to Rodney Crowell (much like "May the force be with you") was mainstream.

Free albums were not the only benefit of working at the radio station. Other freebies included tickets to concerts and sporting events. The Portland Trailblazers, hot off the heels of a world championship, had the hottest ticket in town. Getting courtside seats required working the game.

Our new radio station had a new news department. Gregg Hersholt, a relative newcomer to the business from a small radio station in Spokane, was named station news director. Gregg was overwhelmed trying to find a home and move his family from Spokane. I used the opportunity to help reduce his workload. I offered to take a tape machine to Blazer games, and bring back interviews with Blazer coach Jack Ramsey.

Well, as the story goes, one thing led to another. It wasn't long before I began to join the post-game press conferences. Gregg got the biggest kick out of how Dr. Ramsey addressed me every time I asked a question.

"Well, Paul," he always began, and then proceeded to answer the question.

Though we'd only known each other a few days during the Trailblazer rookie camp, Ramsey had a clear disdain for what he considered silly questions about basketball from the media. I sat quietly in the back of the room as he berated reporters from *The Oregonian*.

"None of you have ever been on the court or played the sport. You have no idea what it's like," he would state angrily, in defense of his players.

Since I had seen action on his court and many others, Dr. Jack Ramsey seemed happy to answer all my questions. Soon, instead of leaving raw tape for Gregg, I began to suggest sound bites. I then became more industrious by returning to the station to edit sound bites. Eventually, I started to leave my sound bites with Associated Press copy, marking where my interviews should be used. The players, meanwhile, started to become more comfortable with me than other members of the media because of our commonality. That, of course, led to even better sound and regular exclusives for the station. By midseason, I began to leave Gregg complete reports that I'd voiced over. To my surprise, Gregg started to use snippets of my reports. By then, he was used to having the best interviews from what was still the biggest game in town.

One morning, I heard myself on the radio. Gregg had used my entire report with no changes. Soon after, I suggested that I should be paid for my extra work. Gregg not only agreed, but hired me as KYTE's first sports director. I suspected the folks at Gaylord Broadcasting in Texas, who had taken a keen interest in me since I was the station receptionist, made the final decision. But it took Gregg to bring me to their attention again.

Gregg was the best boss anyone could ask for. He knew I was green, but he was willing to nurture me. He taught me the tricks of news production. When I was ready, he put me on the air. Suddenly, I was off and running with a promising career in broadcast journalism. To my surprise, I already had one admirer.

Have you ever met someone and thought somehow the two of you could be related? It's rare to find a kindred spirit. George Harris was mine. George was a news reporter for KGW radio, the perennial number one station in Portland.

Just like me, George was the only African-American on staff. In retrospect, he was the only African-American on commercial radio in Portland. So when I showed up at the Trailblazers game with a tape machine in tow, he took great interest in me. George introduced himself to me after the first time he heard me on the air.

"Who is this brother?" he confided to me in later years. He thought my questions were on target, my voice was network quality, and my storytelling skills were rock solid. It was the highest praise I'd ever received from someone in the business.

Of course, I was a member of the mutual admiration society. I admired everything about George. His professionalism and that gregarious laugh that filled the room whenever he was present won me over. Most of all, though, it was his spiffy attire. While I dressed a bit like a Portland State hippie, George wore Harris Tweed jackets like a uniform. I admired George and tried my best to emulate his reporting skills as they applied to speed and deadlines. George had the ability to turn a story, be it sports or news, quickly and effortlessly. I learned this early on after we'd agreed to meet for drinks after a Blazers game.

"I'll meet you at the VQ in an hour," he said.

"An hour?" I thought. "There's no way I can get to the station and leave two reports and a sound bite for the morning news team in one hour." What George could accomplish in less than one hour took me at least three. I agonized over every word and sound bite. George, on the other hand, sat in front of a typewriter and spit out the events that transpired in five minutes.

George and I were like two peas in a pod. It felt like I'd known him forever. I began to look upon him as a brother.

Don't get me wrong. He was still the competition (the one to beat, if you will), and my goal was always to have a better report. But it was a friendly competition. Besides, in the field we rarely let one another out of our sight, as neither one of us wanted the other to get the upper hand in the form of a better or unexpected interview. Once I watched my friend pull his microphone from the podium and rush away from the press conference. He hid in the corner of an industrial complex at the edge of the Willamette River. I followed, asking, "What are you doing?"

"Getting natural sound," he whispered.

Natural sound was a relatively new concept in radio news reporting, one I readily embraced, along with high standards for crystal-clear recordings. I used studio-quality microphones for all my interviews, and now thanks to George, I would layer my reports with relevant ambient sound. The squeaking of tennis shoes on a hardwood floor. The *swoosh* sound a basketball makes as it rips through the net, or nature sounds like the gentle babbling of a brook.

My radio station was still growing. Gaylord hired a new general manager. For whatever reason, he didn't like my boss's style. Gregg was promptly fired. His replacement was quick to let me know that he wanted me gone in the worst way. But by then, I'd become a favorite of the Gaylord Broadcasting boys in Texas; I'd appeared in the company magazine and station newsletter. The Blazers love me, as did the Portland Winter Hawks hockey team, and the city's minor-league baseball team. Firing me would be problematic, so my new boss made my life as difficult as possible, pointing out my insufficiencies, which were many.

Part of me didn't blame him. I was slower than the rest of the staff and had a lot to learn. My typing skills were almost nonexistent. As hard as I tried, other members of the news staff could perform twice as fast as me on my best day.

On the morning of May 18, 1980, my new news director had bigger fish to fry. Nearby Mount St. Helens had erupted with the force of twenty-four megatons of thermal energy, the equivalent to 1,600 times the size of the atomic bomb dropped on Hiroshima, Japan during World War II. The initial eruption sent a column of smoke and ash 80,000 feet into the atmosphere.

It was all hands on deck in the news department. The coverage was extraordinary. Our traffic reporter, Captain Clay Gordon, wasted no time in getting his fixed-wing Cessna up and over Mount St. Helens for a firsthand glimpse. His brave reporting was captivating, as he described the sheer devastation around the mountain. Forty-eight hours later, the mountain was still active, but our news staff was too exhausted to continue such extensive coverage.

I was told to grab a tape machine and head to the U.S. Geological Survey headquarters in Vancouver, Washington. When I arrived, I was mortified by the number of reporters. I set my microphone at the podium and listened intently as scientists began to explain what was happening within the mountain. Suddenly, a strange feeling befell me; any embarrassment for my perceived ineptitude as a sports reporter covering news quickly dissipated.

To most of the reporters in the room that day, the geologist might as well have been speaking Mandarin. I, on the other hand, was able to translate every geologic term. It was at that moment I had the twinkle of knowing that leaving Portland State basketball had been the right decision for me. What a strange thought to have in the midst of such a catastrophic event.

Just like at Los Angeles Harbor Community College, with basketball off my plate, I had immersed myself into my college coursework with reckless abandon. I found earth sciences (which were a heavy part of my senior year course load), particularly geology, fascinating. I'd learned the geologic makeup of the region on class field trips. And most of the scientific terms were still top of mind. So when the geologists began to explain how the cryptodome (the bulge on the mountain) had reached critical mass, so to speak, I knew what they were talking about: a clear precursor to the catastrophic eruption that claimed fifty-seven lives. The term pyroclastic flow was also tucked away in my mind from those courses. Superheated volcanic ash and gases that were capable of traveling down the mountain at supersonic speeds. In the case of Mount St. Helens, the pyroclastic flow flashed boiled water in nearby Spirit Lake, creating a secondary explosion that was heard as far away as British Columbia.

When I completed my first live report from USGS Headquarters, sports suddenly seemed ancillary. At that moment, I lost my lifelong desire to be a disc jockey and set about the task of becoming a news reporter…a journalist, if you will.

When the radio station ordered new business cards to reflect another change in format, my title was changed. Instead of Sports Director, my new business cards simply read Sports/News Reporter. I didn't get to hand out too many of those shiny business cards. My former boss and good friend, Gregg Hersholt, had landed on his feet. He was named news director of KJR in Seattle. What a charmed life for the man whom, coincidently, was the grandson of actor Jean Hersholt. Jean Hersholt is perhaps best known for playing Shirley Temple's grandfather in the movie *Heidi*. The Academy of Motion Picture Arts and Sciences honored him by placing his name on its humanitarian award.

Gregg never spoke of his connection to that Hollywood legacy. However, once while we were both vacationing in Los Angeles, we met up at Sunset Beach for an afternoon of body surfing. At the end of a day of sun, sand, big waves, and beach volleyball, it was time for Gregg to return to his grandmother's digs in Brentwood. "I would love to invite you, but she just wouldn't understand," he sadly confided.

"No big deal," I said, trying to conceal my disappointment. Inside, I was heartbroken. The race issue was slapping me in the face again. A large black man would frighten her, he explained.

I thought, "It's high time for people with racist attitudes to be frightened." I wondered whether Heidi's kindly old grandfather harbored racist attitudes as well. But thought (by virtue of Gregg's actions, his first order of business at KJR would be to hire me as the station's new sports director) that he did not.

"*The 'Seattle Times* did a great story about you," Gregg informed me after the fact. "Oh, and by the way," he said. "We changed your name to Johnson."

I thought he was kidding. But apparently, KJR had a DJ on staff named J.J. Jackson. Though Jackson was not his real name, station management believed that having two Jacksons on staff would confuse the listeners. And so I became Paul Johnson, KJR Sports.

My success in sports immediately translated to the larger market. Lenny Wilkins, head coach of the Seattle Supersonics and one of the NBA's only black coaches, took me under his wing. I'm sure the reasons were twofold. Number one and most obvious: I was a young African-American, a virtual oddity to the business in 1980. And number two: I had a relationship with one of the players responsible for bringing a world championship to the Emerald City, former Harbor College teammate Dennis Johnson. I'm sure playing with DJ gave me instant credibility.

Soon after my arrival, Dennis was traded to the Phoenix Suns. By then, Dennis was an NBA All-Star. His reputation as a hothead preceded him. But, as I learned at Portland State, the better you can play, the more your bad behavior is accepted. And DJ could play! He went on to lead Phoenix to the Pacific Division Title, and his star was still on the rise.

Not long after settling into day-to-day life in Seattle, Gregg offered some unsolicited news I found troubling. It seemed that Verl Wheeler, my station general manager in Portland, was friends with Shannon Sweat, my new general manager at KJR. As the story goes, Wheeler called KJR to chat with his buddy. Sweat was in a meeting with his department heads, but since they were buddies, he took the call. Wheeler was momentarily placed on speakerphone.

"Shannon, Verl here…. You stole my nigger."

The room went silent, and Wheeler was taken off speakerphone.

My heart sank as I looked at Gregg in disbelief. The words stung. Searching for truth, I looked into the eyes of the station's production director Jim Kampmann, who'd also heard the call. Jim did not speak, but simply nodded his head to say *yes*, it was true.

It was not the first time I'd been called nigger. While participating in a weekend survival trip in Death Valley with my Boy Scout troop from Carson, two hunters with high-powered rifles used the word while threatening to kill us. Ray Flowers had a belly laugh at their expense, making fun after they fired and missed their prey a few hundred yards from us.

The N-word was used again in reference to murder after walking across a property that bordered Camp Bishop Stevens in Julian, California, where I spent my summers as a camp counselor. "The next time they cross my property, you're gonna have some dead niggers." Property owner Howard Sprague personally relayed that message to our camp directors.

I heard students in the stands hurl the N word at Freeman Williams during a Portland State basketball game at the University of Puget Sound.

And at a country music concert in Oregon, sponsored by the radio station I worked for, the word was used when I was petting a ferret that had perched on his owner's shoulder. The man looked up and said, "You're a tall nigger." It was one of many torturous events in my life when I felt as if I should've lashed out. Instead, I did nothing.

As a child, I could not figure out Martin Luther King, Jr. It was confusing to watch black people take that much physical abuse in the South during the civil rights movement without lifting a finger in defense or to retaliate. I remember watching as the events in Selma unfolded. I vowed that if that ever happened to me, I would fight back to the death. But when the words were spoken, at least in the case of the man with the ferret, I simply assumed he was so ignorant he just didn't know better.

But Verl Wheeler was no country bumpkin, and his words cut to the bone.

I'd long been under the impression that Wheeler respected me for rising from the mailroom to the newsroom. He shielded me from my new boss, and always treated me fairly. But his words confirmed what I had feared. I was simply a product of affirmative action. I was a mere statistic; our diverse staff was necessary to keep a broadcast license by appeasing the Federal Communications Commission.

His words made me even happier to be in Seattle, where I spent a glorious year at KJR, hobnobbing with the likes of baseball legend Maury Wills, who managed the Mariners. I struck up a friendship with Seahawks quarterback Jim Zorn, a born-again Christian who loved the Lord more than football. But my closest professional confidant remained the great Lenny Wilkins. As an inquisitive young reporter, I once pressed him for an answer to a question he didn't feel comfortable answering. In a final attempt to get a response, I asked in a giddy sort of way, "Can you tell me off the record?" He gave me a stern look and said nothing.

At the conclusion of his press availability, he asked me to remain. When the locker room cleared, he tore into me. "Why would you say 'off the record' in a room full of reporters? Do you think it would be off the record for them?" I understood this was Wilkins's way of telling me to be more professional. I was in the big time, but I was still behaving like a green reporter. Feeling I got the message, he sent me on my way a little wiser.

Meanwhile, broadcast history was about to repeat itself. Once again, Gregg found himself on the outs with management and was demoted from news director to news anchor. Our new news director was B.R. Bradberry, whom I'd listen to as a child in L.A. Soon after he was promoted, Bradberry replaced me with someone more to his liking.

Radio was starting to feel like a revolving door. As the lyrics to the popular television show *WKRP in Cincinnati* go, I began an odyssey that took me "Town to town, up and down the dial."

After returning to Portland, where I was a general assignment reporter at KGW radio, I fell in love, got engaged to local radio personality Carolyn Myers, lost my job, was offered a position in Denver, Colorado, and took it. My fiancée remained in Oregon.

CHAPTER 19

POLITICALLY CONNECTED

My arrival in the Mile-High City was not an auspicious occasion. I drove into Colorado during the grips of winter. I found the icy landscape intimidating. I was anxious behind the wheel since these driving conditions were new to me. The sides of the roads were layered with ugly brown snow, the likes of which I'd never seen. "How could snow be brown?" I wondered. "How dismal. What have I done?"

My new employer, KLIR-FM 100, was gracious enough to put me up at the Doubletree Hotel until I could find a permanent place to hang my hat. The Mile-High City certainly outshone its name, pilfering my breath, stealing my strength, and drying my skin. As I struggled into the lobby with my luggage, I couldn't help but wonder how I ever left Oregon.

The next day, I reported to the station to meet with KLIR's new business manager. He was a young Hispanic man, and I liked him immediately. He was sincere and welcoming. In fact, it would not be a stretch to say he seemed ecstatic I'd arrived. He struck me as the kind of guy who appreciated a bit of diversity on the airwaves. While that may have been the case, I soon found that wasn't the reason he gave me such a warm greeting. Turns out he was much more excited about me being 6'10" and possessing some basketball skills. He wasted no time in recruiting me for his club team. Actually, he begged me to join them in a game that evening.

So, on my second day in Denver, I thought it prudent to join the team. I found myself engaged in a high-stakes game of AAU basketball, gasping for air at altitude. I still possessed enough leg strength to make my presence felt on the court. The team was a group of business professionals from the Denver area. The game was fiercely competitive, but thanks in part to me, we were winning handily. I recall it was late in the fourth quarter. I'd screened out a much smaller player on defense. I was ready to go up after a rebound when a teammate, all alone, went sky-high and grabbed the ball.

"Nice rebound," I thought to myself, while he contorted his body as if an NBA All-Star were trying to steal his ball. He was a prominent Denver attorney who stood about 6'4", weighed about 230 pounds, and looked to be in decent shape. As he came to the ground, he hurled his elbows soundly, cracking me in my nose, and shaking me to my knees. He threw the outlet pass, apparently never realizing the damage he'd done. When I tried to stand and shake it off, blood poured profusely from my nose. I knew instantly; my nose was broken.

The business manager took me to the nearest emergency room, where the attending ER physician told me, "Yep, your nose is broken. There's really nothing we can do for a broken nose. You just have to see how it sets."

I went back to the Doubletree, where I collapsed into my bed, dried blood and all. It seemed no sooner had my head hit the pillow than the hotel phone began to ring. "Hello, Mr. Jackson. This is your five o'clock wake-up call."

"Thank you," I said, groggily. I was late for my first day on the air.

Although I did not display my usual extraordinary vocal clarity that day, it seemed no one knew I was broadcasting with a broken nose. And everyone (except me, of course) was pleased with my on-air presence.

Thanks to longtime family friends, I became politically connected in Denver. In addition, my fiancée's father, Clay Myers, a long-time Oregon politician, insisted I meet his Colorado counterpart, who happened to be one of his dearest friends. And so I was invited to the office of Roy Romer, Colorado's State Treasurer, whom I found to be most affable. He said he was sorry he wouldn't be able to introduce me to the governor, who was not in his office. I was actually relieved. I'd met Governor Richard Lamm on two previous occasions, and frankly, he made me a bit nervous.

At our second meeting (the Western Governors' Conference in Oregon), I approached him for an interview. I began by saying, "Hello, Governor Lamm. I'm Paul Jackson from KGW radio. I don't know if you remember me."

The governor interrupted and proceeded to give me a sharp tongue-lashing. "Of course I remember you," he replied in a loud, annoyed tone. He spoke to me as if I'd just called him an idiot. I don't recall his tirade word for word, but it had to do with me being almost seven feet tall, so how could I ask such a silly question? How could he possibly forget me, or how could *anyone* forget me? Or something to that effect.

Touché, Governor. I suppose there aren't that many seven-foot African-American reporters covering Western governors. I suppose I should have been flattered that he remembered.

I had a long visit with the state treasurer, who went on to become Colorado's thirty-ninth Governor. He extended his warmest platitudes and a not-always-customary, "If there's anything I can do for you, just give me a call."

~~~

A few months later, the distance and my fiancée's inability to find work in the Denver radio market led her to call off the engagement, and we ended our relationship. But her family, especially her father, will forever hold a special place in my heart.

I never expected her dad to accept us. And...I've never been so wrong about anything. The fact is that he warmly and completely accepted me, with no regard for the potential political fallout. He not only showed me something about the kind of man he was, but he also gave me hope that, because of people like him, the cycle of hate and racial prejudice in our country was breakable. He made my transition to Colorado easier, and even came to check on me in my crummy apartment in Denver.

My biggest regret about him haunts me to this day. When he was Oregon State Treasurer, the Black United Front in Portland lambasted him for a trip he took to South Africa during the time of apartheid. I was pulled from another story to cover the hastily-called press conference. When the organization's founder, Ron Herndon, announced the reason for the press conference, I should have excused myself for being too close to the story to file an objective report. I also had another option. I could have interrupted the event and spoken up before it became an all-out attack on this man's integrity. Clay Myers did travel to South Africa, but not as a representative of the State of Oregon. He was there on behalf of the Episcopal Church to visit Bishop Desmond Tutu, the Anglican cleric known for his opposition to apartheid in South Africa.

I knew of the meeting and purpose of his visit, which was to offer support to the cause. The fact I never spoke up about the actual reason he was in the country and the kind of man I knew him to be makes me ashamed. In truth, I was paralyzed with fear that I would be ridiculed since tensions at the event were high. I was simply too young and inexperienced as a journalist to take control and speak up in his defense. I wish I had the kind of courage Clay Myers possessed.

He could've defended himself by using me as an example, saying, "Look, I'm not prejudiced, and I don't support apartheid. My daughter is engaged to a black man." But he did not. Clay Myers passed away in 2004. During his political career, he was considered one of Oregon's most influential moderate Republicans. Following his death, he was honored in a joint resolution of the Oregon state legislature as "a gentle but tenacious leader who cared deeply about making Oregon a more livable and just place, and whose strong faith and unwavering efforts helped make Oregon a national model." I simply choose to remember him as a good man.

I had a blast doing morning drive time news in Denver. I chose my own assignments and used the afternoons to get out and pick up interviews. I'd attend the mayor's weekly press conference, which was always entertaining. The city's new mayor was creating quite a buzz. He was young, single, and Denver's first Hispanic mayor, which instantly made Federico Peña the nation's most eligible bachelor.

Peña's weekly news conferences typically took place in his office conference room, where he sat at the table with reporters and issued a well-scripted news statement. Then he took questions from the media. When I looked at the young brown man leading our city, I felt proud to be a minority. Our media sessions were usually non-adversarial. Pena was articulate, accommodating, good-natured, and the darling of the media. President Bill Clinton later tapped him to become the U.S. Secretary of Transportation.

I had a ready-made family in Denver. Rosemary Berry had been my aunt Dazelle's college roommate. She was like a second sister to my aunt, which instantly made me family. Mr. Berry was a kindhearted soul who suffered from, and later succumbed to, multiple sclerosis. Like Aunt Dazelle, the Berrys were a family of means, and they owned several properties throughout Denver. They had three children. Elease was a professor at the University of Colorado; Alan was a college recruiter; and Leslie was a civil servant with political aspirations. I hung out with Les whenever I could. He was a matter-of-fact brother who didn't talk slang and was generally a joy to be around. He often invited me to his condo for the pleasure of company and dinner with him and his family since I was new to town. It wasn't long before I realized his was a high-end condominium where tenants went far beyond rock star status.

"Oh yeah, Pat lives over there, and Gary lives upstairs," Les told me of his neighbors. The Pat he was referring to was Congresswoman Patricia Schroeder, and the guy upstairs turned out to be Senator Gary Hart, who was about to begin his campaign for the presidency of The United States.

I visited Leslie often and soon became friends with Congresswoman Patricia Schroeder. She loved to talk with me at poolside. Over time, she felt she knew me well enough to give me her personal feelings on the President of the United States. What she told me was quite frightening.

"You can tell him one thing one minute, and he'll forget it the next. He doesn't remember anything," she confided. Pat Schroeder, who would later become the first woman to run for President as a legitimate candidate, apparently sensed early on that Ronald Reagan suffered from some sort of dementia while in office. To hear her tell it, Nancy Reagan had to act as commander-in-chief on numerous occasions. Reagan later disclosed that he had been diagnosed with Alzheimer's Disease while he was in office. Turns out Pat Schroeder's poolside disclosure about a man who should not have had his finger on the nuclear trigger was right on target.

More important issues than the security of the United States of America were discussed poolside. I soon found myself attracted to a gorgeous brunette, and she seemed to be checking me out as well. Our flirtation went on for a few weeks. I finally worked up the courage to meet her and ask her out. As I began to make my move, Leslie asked me, "You see those dudes on the roof with machine guns?"

"Yeah," I replied.

"You've been flirting with Gary's daughter."

While I was attracted to her, I found my courage waning. The Secret Service security detail assigned to protect candidate Gary Hart dissuaded me from asking her out on a date. A little voice inside my head said a tryst with a black man could jeopardize the senator's presidential aspirations. But mostly, it was the guys with machine guns on the roof.

CHAPTER 20

A LOST CHILD

Like a salmon swimming upstream, I eventually made it back to God's country—Eugene, Oregon. It was 1985, and I was the new hire at KPNW Radio, a 50,000-watt AM and FM powerhouse that covered Western Oregon. I was the news director, and I supervised a staff of two.

At the time, Eugene was a white enclave where the small minority population ebbed and flowed annually, depending on the number of scholarships given to minority athletes by the University of Oregon.

The station hired me, sight unseen, on the strength of the demonstration tape I submitted. The entire interview process took place over the telephone (I lived in Denver and worked part-time for KOA radio, the number-one news talk station). With no prospect of full-time employment on the horizon, I "shopped" my tape across the country.

When I arrived at KPNW radio for my first day of work, I got the distinct feeling my boss didn't know he had hired a black man. The station manager's visual astonishment meant little to me. At 6'10", I was used to receiving stares. I was delighted to be back in the state I had come to call home after spending most of my college years at Portland State University, less than two hours away.

Any fears station management might have had about hiring a black man were quickly put to rest after my first broadcast. The program director burst into the newsroom to compliment my style. It seemed my new general manager liked my "big-city sound." This meant his neck was temporarily out of the noose for hiring a black man. It was clear I brought credibility to KPNW's on-air sound. I assumed it was the start of a long and lasting relationship, and it may very well have been, had it not been for a vivacious DJ I will call Franny Pack.

Back then, there were simple rules to surviving in small towns. Do what you're told. Don't make waves; and, whatever you do, don't date white women. Well, I was about to break some rules.

The moment I laid eyes on her, I knew trouble was afoot. Franny was a tall, shapely woman with a bright smile and easy style. Anyone who met her was attracted to her magnetic personality; her warmth came across to the listeners. That made her the number-one DJ in the market's evening time slot.

When I arrived in Eugene, Franny had just separated from her husband. She was the object of intense interest from almost every man at the station, including my boss. While I could elicit a smile of interest, it was clear Franny was doing her level best to start an office romance with Greg Oberst, the station's production director. I was privy to this juicy bit of gossip because Greg and I were close friends. He was a recent University of Oregon graduate whose father owned a radio station along the Oregon coast. As a result, Greg grew up in the business and seemed ready to leave small-town USA to make his mark in the big city. Despite Franny's hot pursuit, Greg showed no interest. After briefly questioning his sanity, I felt it was my duty as his new best friend to encourage him to pursue Franny. When he declined, I wasted no time in positioning myself as the logical runner-up. I was a bit surprised when Franny eagerly accepted my advances, but even more so when I picked her up for our first date and discovered she had three young children: two girls and a boy. The shock quickly subsided as I discovered what amazing human beings they were.

Franny's children were clean slates with no prejudices, and a sense of wonder about everything. It was my first time around children, and I was surprised to find myself bonding with the youngest, a four-year-old girl with golden hair and inquisitive eyes. She followed me around their home. The first time I picked her up, she flashed a bright smile, creating a sense of warmth and joy that washed over me. As if by magic, the loneliness that had consumed my life washed away, and I instantly knew why people wanted children. Franny and her family filled a void in life I never realized existed until that magical moment with her youngest daughter.

As days turned to weeks, our casual relationship became more serious. Being with Franny brought me intense pleasure, physically and emotionally. She must have felt the same because she introduced me to her mother, father, and sister. I even accompanied her on a weekend trip to her parents' home at the foot of Mount Hood. I went skiing and returned late that evening to avoid any family conflicts that might arise because of my presence. But when I returned, I found Franny's mother had prepared a family dinner for us. Her father, a rotund man, seemed eager to talk with me and welcomed me into their home.

Despite my growing affection for Franny's family, a cautionary voice deep within constantly warned I could not have a serious relationship with a woman who was raising three young children. Still, the intense attraction remained.

On one particularly passionate night, we gazed at each other in silence and then continued our lovemaking. The chain of events that followed remains forever burned into my mind. The room began to change colors. More correctly, it became devoid of color. It changed to what I can only describe as a grainy gray that appeared to flicker and move like the background of an old black-and-white film. The air became heavy and still. All background noise seemed to disappear. Then, what I can only describe as entities from another realm entered my bedroom from three sides: the window, the wall, and ceiling. Whatever energy form was present seemed to float inside my body, taking some of my mental faculties. I remember looking up, unable to focus my eyes or figure out what was happening to me. All I felt was the existence of another being in my room. A few seconds later, I felt the force leave my body and perceived it to enter Franny, who seemed unaware of the phenomena. I instantly knew what had happened.

Franny was pregnant.

I lay there, temporarily stunned, unable to move, and unwilling to speak. I knew I had to keep what I'd experienced to myself. It was the first of three psychic events I experienced over the course of the next nine months. Nothing could prepare me for what was about to happen.

Once Franny realized what I had known for weeks, she immediately made the decision not to terminate her pregnancy. She confided in me that she'd had an abortion some years before, and the aftermath left her guilt-ridden and distraught. Since she could not endure the remorse of ending the pregnancy, her path was clear. I felt overjoyed by her decision, for I had also experienced the trauma of abortion, years earlier, when my college sweetheart ended an unwanted pregnancy, against my wishes. I intended to support Franny, but tears rolled down her cheeks when I told her I didn't want to get married.

Several weeks into her pregnancy, Franny failed to show up for work. When I called to check on her, she said she wasn't feeling well and needed to rest. I intuitively felt something was terribly wrong and rushed to her house. When I arrived, Franny was running a high fever. Against her wishes, I insisted we go to the hospital. I remember the doctor calling me into the emergency room, and then turning to Franny to ask whether I was the father. Ever cheerful, she managed a broad smile, and, nodding yes, she managed to laugh.

A sense of pride washed over me. Our secret was out; Franny and I were having a child together. As she fought to hold back tears, the ER doctor's grave look arrested the moment. Pulling me aside, he told me that if I had not brought Franny in exactly when I did, the baby would have died. Franny's fever had reached 104 degrees. I cared for Franny and her family for the rest of the week, delivering hot soup and fluids. The experience drew me even closer to them. I wanted to be with her more than ever, but I still felt that fathering four children would be impossible. Looking back, I now realize how selfish I was.

After Franny recovered, I wondered, "How did I know my child's life was in danger, and why was I compelled to act at that moment?" The answer is clear; this life was preordained. It chose us, and it called out to me as it had during the night of its supernatural conception.

By this point in our relationship, Franny's oldest daughter had begun to miss her father desperately, and she blamed me for his absence. I knew little about him, other than what I heard from Franny and her friends. According to Franny, Dave was an irresponsible musician, and she had asked him to leave. Still, this little girl missed her daddy, and she told me so as often as possible. It soon became clear she didn't want me around her mother. I felt I had no chance to win her over. My deeper sense was that I could never hope to (nor did I want to) replace her father.

With all this drama playing out, I asked Franny if she would consider living with me with her youngest daughter and our child, and allow her oldest daughter and son to live with their father. This was a complete reversal from our no-strings-attached relationship—in my mind, a quantum leap closer to marriage. While the query seemed logical and innocent enough to me, I was utterly oblivious to the magnitude of what I asked until many years later. I wanted Franny to break up her family for me.

Unaware of my stupidity, I was reasonably certain that Franny and I would co-exist in some sort of relationship. I decided it was time to fly home to Los Angeles to give my family the news. I felt obligated to tell my mother because I would surely need her support in raising a child.

My mother reacted with shock and dismay. She tried to talk me out of it. Raised in the Deep South in the time of Jim Crow, she viewed interracial relationships with fear and disdain. She tried for two days to talk me out of my decision. I had not come home for advice. I'd returned home to deliver the news out of love and respect for my mother. With that same love, she, with much skepticism, accepted my decision and pledged support should I need it.

With the burden of telling my family lifted, I returned to Eugene with a sense of pride and excitement. My flight had a brief layover in San Francisco. The stop turned into a long weather delay, as heavy fog shrouded the region. Not wanting to inconvenience Franny, who was going to pick me up at the airport, I called to let her know my flight was delayed. I will never forget the words that followed.

"I'll pick you up," she said in a low voice. "But you won't like the news." Over the course of my three-day weekend, Franny had not only reconciled with her husband, but she had allowed him to return home. They had already formulated a plan. I could take the child at birth or let them raise it. In shock, I weighed my options. I sincerely wanted to raise my child. However, I felt a child needs a mother, and I knew what a wonderful mother Franny was. I had no idea what to do. It felt like a two-ton weight had been dropped on my chest, and the pressure to choose was crushing me. You see, somewhere along the line, I'd fallen in love with Franny. Unfortunately, I'd never told her, and now it was too late. Any attempt at winning her back, at least in my mind, was morally wrong. After all, she was married.

Franny never told me why she let Dave back into her life, but I knew it was a repercussion of my suggesting she tear her family apart.

When I returned to work, Franny was conspicuously absent. I soon learned that despite her dazzling on-air performance and top ratings (the highest at the station), she had been called into the general manager's office and fired on the spot. I was not privy to the reasons, but it is safe to assume she was let go for dating me and becoming pregnant with my child. The news of her departure shocked everyone at the station. I felt responsible and fell into a deep, depressive funk.

With Franny out of my life, I distracted myself with sports. I joined an AAU basketball team to pass the time. The competition was fierce, as the league was filled with former NCAA players who remained in Eugene after college. This forced me to bring my A-Game. Shooting hoops became more than exercise. Every move became physical combat, which proved to be a great release for my frustrations.

One evening while driving toward the basket for a sure slam-dunk, I heard a loud pop resonate through my body. I was surprised when no one looked over to see where the noise came from. Then I realized it was the sound of my knee. I excused myself from the game, believing I had simply pulled something. It was a bit painful, but I didn't give it much thought. When the game was over and it was time to leave, I climbed into my car and tried to raise my right leg to the pedals. Nothing. I had no muscular control. I was still somewhat unconcerned, and a teammate offered to chauffeur me home.

The next day, Greg was kind enough to take me to the doctor. Since I could not bend my leg, he helped me into the bed of his compact pick-up truck. Once at the hospital, I soon learned I had done a little more than pull something. Following my initial examination, the doctor ushered in a large group of interns. It seems I was a bit of a medical oddity. "Look at this," the doctor told the group. "This guy severed his patella tendon yesterday, and just came in for treatment." Apparently, the pain of such an injury was so excruciating that any "normal person" would've gone to the hospital immediately. I, on the other hand, had spent my life playing through the pain, until pain became a way of life, a low-level annoyance. I had no idea my tendon was slowly tearing away.

I learned I would require immediate surgery before the muscles could retract, making it impossible to reconnect the tendon to the bone. If that happened, I would be permanently handicapped. The doctor told me very little of the surgical procedure other than I had a 90 percent chance of a 90 percent recovery, meaning my knee could be repaired, but it would never be the same. My surgeon neglected to tell me that they might have to remove tissue from my calf to reconnect the tendon.

Fortunately, my surgery went smoothly and the worst-case scenario didn't happen. Still, I faced a three- to four-month recovery period, after which I was strongly advised never to play basketball again.

The day after surgery, I refused pain medication. But the extraordinary tolerance of pain I spoke of earlier was about to change. I have no idea what it feels like to be shot, nor do I wish to find out. But I can only imagine it has to rival the pain I felt the first time I stood erect after surgery. The blood flew to all parts of my leg. First a twinge, then throbbing, followed by unimaginable agony. From that moment, I timed my allotted dose of morphine with physical activity.

The first stages of rehabilitation were demoralizing. I could barely walk, and I lost the ability to drive. My mother, who had flown up to assist me, even had to help me put on my underwear. During her stay with me, we discussed my unborn child and my desire to raise the baby. My mother's uneasy feelings reemerged. "Leave that family alone!" she said. "If they want to raise the child, for God's sake, let them! You're off the hook."

There I was, virtually crippled, and in my deepest time of need, my own flesh and blood refused to help me raise my child. It was the first time I can remember my mother refusing to help me with anything. Her refutation added to my guilt about Franny.

Having only work to look forward to, I rushed back to the radio station weeks ahead of my scheduled return, propped my leg on a chair, and began to do my newscast. I felt like a hero, a model employee coming to the station's rescue, putting its wellbeing above my own. At the end of my shift, someone called me into the general manager's office, and I was promptly fired. No reason was given, but I knew it was because of my relationship with Franny.

Now unemployed, and temporarily crippled, I faced the bleak realization that there was simply no way I could care for a newborn baby. Hell, I couldn't even tie my shoes. My family flatly refused to help, imploring me to leave Franny's family alone. But I could not. My child was still communicating with me.

My last communication with my unborn child came one night in late June. I woke up in a cold sweat, knowing everything. As Franny's due date drew near, I was consumed with the thought of mother and child. I somehow sensed Franny was in turmoil. I, on the other hand, felt tranquility wash over and through me. Miraculously, just as I knew the moment the baby was conceived, I instantaneously knew when it would be born. Furthermore, I knew her sex. I felt I needed to alleviate Franny's fears so she could experience what I was feeling. I picked up the phone and a voice inside me instructed me to say, "I know you are worried. I know you are overdue, but the baby is fine. It's a girl, and she will be born on the fourth of July."

When Franny answered the phone, I realized how insane it might have sounded to her. I listened quietly to her voice on the other end of the line. "Hello."

I waited to reply, as I sensed she knew it was me. She said hello again, waited, listened silently, and then hung up.

On July 4, 1986, Morgan Pack was born. Four days later, I received a terse letter from Dave and Franny, warning me to stay away. They wrote, "We firmly insist that you cease your efforts to contact any member of our family. If you will not respect our wishes, we are prepared to take whatever legal action necessary to ensure our privacy." After that letter, they literally went into hiding, cutting off all contact with mutual friends and acquaintances.

My family and most of my friends continued to advise me to stay away from the Pack family. My sisters showed unexpected respect for Franny's husband, saying that any man who could accept another man's child, especially a black man's child, into his family was extraordinary. Male friends considered me lucky because Franny didn't sue for child support. I, on the other hand, prayed for any contact, and consulted with anyone who might offer advice. To preserve my sanity, I began to journal and eventually wrote a letter to Morgan.

CHAPTER 21

A LETTER TO MORGAN

Dear Morgan,

Obsessed with your existence, I went to confront your family. When I knocked on the front door, I discovered the house was empty. They had moved away, obtained an unlisted phone number, and vanished. I searched for you, but no one knew where your family had gone. Months later, your mother emerged as an on-air personality at Eugene's number-one radio station. We talked by phone and she told me she wanted me to meet you, but David was against it. She told me a little about who you were and how you were growing up. She said you were a blessing to the family, and that you somehow brought them all together. While this gave me some peace of mind, I felt it was my God-given right to be a part of your life.

When it was clear there was no other course of action to take, I retained a lawyer. Our strategy was to strong-arm your family into granting me contact by threatening messy legal action. Your mother was still the top jock at the radio station, where she continued to command a loyal following. We believed she would not want this issue aired in public. Deep inside, I believed your mom wanted me to have contact with you (at least that is what she told my lawyer) because my intent was not custody, but visitation. We later learned it was subterfuge, to placate us with a promise of a face-to-face conference, while Dave was secretly filing papers to adopt you.

The Oregon Department of Human Resources, Children's Services Division added the final insult by accepting the adoption without an investigation. On March 6, 1989, the Lane County Circuit Court in Oregon concluded, "Paternity has not been established, and there are no other proceedings pending for that purpose, so notice to or consent from the child's putative father was not required." In a twisted web of lies, Franny and Dave committed perjury by contending I had abandoned you and could not be located. The adoption was sealed.

I continued to pursue my parental rights for years to come, sending you birthday cards and Christmas presents. At one point, I even drove one-thousand miles and ambushed your mom, showing up unannounced at her radio station. Oddly, it was her birthday. We embraced and had a brief private meeting where she told me that she thought it was important for me to have contact with you. She gave me a picture of you that I carry with me to this day. She said she shared her feelings with your father, but he would simply not allow me access.

To Dave, I was the man who tore apart his family, and it was his turn to dispense justice. Years later, I learned just how much he hated me, when he sent a letter to my wife detailing my perceived offenses against his family. I, on the other hand, had come to respect him for the true father he had become to you. In my opinion, he was a better man than I could ever hope to be for taking in another man's child, but I was still not willing to let you go.

Eight years after your birth, I had a promising career as a television journalist and was in love with Amy, the woman who would become my wife and give me two beautiful daughters, your half-sisters: Katelyn Imani and Kyra Skye. I was happier than one man could hope to be in his lifetime, yet I still agonized over a soul that touched my life, but had yet to reveal itself. I still needed to see you; I needed to hear you say, "I am all right, and I have a good life."

At this point, I finally had the financial resources required to mount a full-out effort to gain contact with you. With the aid of Richard Gilbert, a prominent family rights attorney from Southern California, I took my case all the way to the Oregon Supreme Court, fully expecting it to hear the truth. Gilbert wrote, "The primary and only basis for the relief sought by plaintiff is that he is…the father…."

On December 7, 1994, the high court affirmed, without opinion, the lower court's decision that denied my parental right. The circle of lies was complete, as the courts turned a blind eye to the truth.

I know times change and perceptions of African-American men are gradually beginning to shift. But I am reasonably certain that stereotypically, black men are still viewed in most circles as absentee parents. Immoral men who have little regard for the parenting process. It is generally assumed we vanish, leaving the woman to go it alone.

When it comes to you, it may have been a lot easier to emulate the stereotype. It would have been less painful than lamenting over a child stolen because of rules that once enacted, cannot be undone.

Martin Luther King, Jr. said, "We must accept finite disappointment, but we must never lose infinite hope."

I may no longer receive psychic messages from you, but I still feel you in my heart and see you in my dreams. Please know that I never intended to hurt anyone. All I wanted was to love you, and I did…and I do. *We are Ohana.*

Love,

Paul, Your Father

With that, I released all expectations, and let go, and let God.

CHAPTER 22

RADICAL FORGIVENESS

Years later, I heard from Morgan. She wanted me to know she was coming to Los Angeles to visit *my mother*. "How is that possible?" I wondered. It could have been the happiest moment of my life, but her letter unleashed a chain of lies more hurtful than the loss of the child herself.

I'd been sending letters to Morgan since she was a child. Eventually, one of them made it past Dave's and Franny's watchful eyes and wound up in her possession. I can imagine it opened a floodgate of questions.

In my letters, I sent information about my family members, so she would know about them in the event of my untimely death. My adventures in the field of news prompted me to do so after learning firsthand that fire could move like water in the wind. Barely escaping the flames, I couldn't help but think that if I stayed this close to danger, it might be just a matter of time before I got burned.

I lived in a fantasy world when it came to Morgan. The truth was that while I considered myself her knight in shining armor, I was in fact the monster children check for in the closet and parents look for under the bed. For her entire life, all she ever heard were stories of me being a villain.

And so it was when it was time for her to reach out to family, her first letters were not to me but to my sisters. Elizabeth received a letter early on. Not only did she fail to mention it to me, but she began a relationship with Morgan, visiting with her and her family at her home in Michigan. Then she took her on a whirlwind tour of Miami to meet our relatives.

My family kept this secret from me for years. It strained my relationship with my mother, who compounded the lie by claiming to have no knowledge. I was humiliated by the fact that the circle of lies could be kept so tightly and long without anyone uttering a word to me.

My sister, Paula, eventually stepped up to end the lies.

Hate is a strong word, but I assume Morgan's family hated me. Part of me could understand their actions. As for Elizabeth, when I confronted her about her relationship with my daughter, she blurted out, "Just because you donated sperm doesn't make you the father."

Now a teen, Morgan had spent her entire life with a family that detested me, and my sister, whom I now know hated me.

I spent years wondering how my sister could do such an insufferable thing. A well-respected psychotherapist from Temple University helped me unravel the truth. "Elizabeth was abused by your father, and your mother did not come to her rescue." Her face wore the pain of an empath, reliving the pain of the moment as she theorized, "Since no one protected Elizabeth from her father, she took it upon herself to protect your daughter from you."

I soaked in this theory for many years. Then one spring, I took a course in radical forgiveness, which taught me that forgiving is not for the purpose of healing the offender, but healing the forgiver. I was finally able to offer Elizabeth my forgiveness.

When I told her this via telephone, there was silence on the line, and then, without a word…the line went dead.

CHAPTER 23

A GLIMPSE

I suppose you've figured out that I'm a bit of a psychic. Sometimes it's little things. For instance, while working in the yard one day, I suddenly grasped a bush, for seemingly no reason, while near a slight drop in my yard. Then, I became aware that I was holding on to the bush for no apparent reason and let go. A moment later, a gust of wind—strong enough to push me off balance—blew through the yard sending me stumbling down the incline. I think we all have the ability to glimpse the future. Some of us are more in tune than are others.

I'd had dozens of unconfirmed psychic episodes, and almost all of them had something to do with nature, usually extreme weather events and, in some cases...earthquakes.

Following the historic eruption of Mount St. Helens on May 18, 1980, I became connected to the mountain. This most bizarre and unusual occurrence in my life couldn't have been more random since I had no inkling the initial eruption was imminent. But as impossible as it may sound, I sensed each subsequent eruption as it occurred in real time. Activity on and around Mount St. Helens continued during the summer and fall of 1980. Each event produced eruption columns eight to nine miles above sea level, and sent pyroclastic flows down the volcano's north face. The mountain was rebuilding itself, and for reasons beyond my understanding, I could feel it happening.

It didn't matter where I was or what I was doing. I would become overcome with emotion, as a look of distress crawled across my face, then swept over my body. After a moment, I'd be back in my body, announcing to anyone in my proximity, "The mountain just erupted."

I can give no reasonable explanation as to why I became in touch or connected with seismic activity. Nor can I claim an unnatural life event like, say, being struck by lightning. Although at some point in my life, lightning did indeed strike me. More about that later.

Sure enough, a check-in on the radio would reveal a major tremor had occurred within the mountain. The larger the harmonic tremor and subsequent eruption, the deeper the knowing within me.

The strongest feelings occurred early on Sunday morning, May 25, 1980, when the mountain blew off most of the lava dome formed after the initial eruption. While that eruption occurred, I somehow experienced it. These eruptions were miles away, so I could not have possibly heard or felt them. The only plausible explanation was I was in touch, in synch, connected, or psychic. Call it what you will. It was a strange gift to have, and one I have not chosen to reveal until now.

This connection to events in nature has continued throughout my life, manifesting in survivalist ways. I once sent my daughters to the basement after I stepped outside one night to empty the trash. When I looked to the sky, it was iridescent, and the wind was almost dead still. I had a "knowing" that sent chills through my body. I escorted my daughters to the safest place in our home, which was a corner of the basement, until my angst subsided. The next morning, I learned that a freak tornado had shredded two blocks in Willow Grove, a community not far from our home.

What I now refer to as "the knowing" began when I was just a child. I recall one such day of consternation. I was convinced the world was coming to an end. Instead of playing hide and seek, I altered my childhood game by telling my playmates to find a safe place to hide with me before the bombs dropped. I nervously scanned the sky for airplanes or missiles. I sprinted about because I didn't want to be caught in the open. I looked for anything to hide under. After cowering all day, I came home to find my parents glued to the television, learning for the first time about the Cuban missile crisis.

I've had several people confirm my psychic ability. My sister Paula has known since we were children. Paula still speaks of my ability to this day. Paula was walking home from Leapwood Avenue Elementary School, as she did every weekday, with the hordes of children who lived in Del Ammo Highlands. The walk was a tad less than two miles as the crow flies. I almost always rode my bicycle to school, but on this particular day, for whatever reason, I decided to walk. I never walked with my sister, as she was usually with her girlfriends. On this particular day, I was alone, dreading the long walk home.

Suddenly, a group of kids rushed past.

"I'm gonna get her," one girl said.

Another chimed in, "Yeah, let's beat her up."

Without them so much as uttering a name, I instinctively knew they were after my sister. I began to run toward home as fast as I could. I caught up with Paula a couple of blocks away. Her happy mood was dashed moments later when the group caught up with us. They followed closely and shoved us from behind, in hopes of provoking a fight. Outnumbered ten to two, we kept walking and managed to make it home safely.

Paula was aware of my ability…my knowing. Following her rescue, she never viewed me in the same light.

CHAPTER 24

CHOPPER 7

Growing up, the only things I loved watching more than trains, planes, and automobiles, heck even rocket ships, were helicopters. When I was young, they were generally referred to as "Whirlybirds," which also happened to be the name of a popular television series I was most taken by. The show (which first aired in 1957) was about two daredevil pilots who owned a helicopter company. They rented out their services and performed various jobs.

Now, like most kids of that era, my television hero was Sky King. "Sky King" was a black-and-white, aerial action adventure about a World War II naval aviator-turned rancher, who flew his twin-engine Cessna high above the Arizona plains. On Saturday mornings, you could find me glued to the television watching Sky King use his airplane, "Songbird," to find lost hikers and foil the capers of countless criminals.

But high above the ground in the Songbird, Sky King could only circle the bad guys. Sure, he could buzz them, but he would eventually have to find a place to land to capture them. The pilot of the whirlybird, on the other hand, could hover above the crooks. In one episode, the whirlybird pilot chased down a bad guy who (of course) tripped and fell. The pilot moved to land the chopper smack dab on the bad guy's chest. It was a controlled hover, of course, so as not to crush or injure him too badly, applying just enough pressure to hold him for authorities. It was the coolest thing I had ever seen.

Following that episode, I gazed into the sky, transfixed, and listened for the distant *pop, pop, pop* of rotor blades. "LOOK! A whirlybird!" I would scream at the top of my lungs, watching in delight and always wishing I were aboard the chopper as it crossed the dry Southern California sky.

If I have not stated it earlier, I do so now, unequivocally: be careful what you wish for.

As a sports reporter for KMGH-TV (second tour) in Denver, I got a plum assignment covering the Coors Classic International Bicycle Race. I was ecstatic when I learned I'd cover the mountain stage of the race from "Chopper 7," a Bell Jet Ranger.

Peter Peelgrane piloted Chopper 7. He was an affable Aussie with a colorful history. Peter was internationally renowned for his flying skill. Prior to arriving in America, he was a captain in the Australian Air Force. Virtually everyone on our news staff loved and admired him and had the utmost confidence in his ability as a pilot.

"You're in good hands," they told me. "He's the best!"

Peelgrane was a member (Who knows, possibly the founder?) of an exclusive club. He inverted his helicopter (as in flying upside down) and lived to tell the tale.

I was full of anticipation as we boarded Chopper 7. I felt perfectly safe. I'd dreamt of flying in a chopper for more than a quarter of a century, and now my dream was about to come true. I was a bit of a tub back then, in fact, the heaviest I'd been in my entire life. After months of relative inactivity following my knee surgery, I'd bloated to the size of a super-heavyweight boxer. I was a couple of Big Macs over 250 pounds.

My photographer, though several inches shorter, was a large man as well. Since we would be in the wilderness, miles from the resources of the station, he boarded the chopper with extra equipment: his camera, tape, a heavy tripod, and extra batteries.

Peter told me to sit in the front seat since I had the longest legs. Unlike an airplane, the passenger seat in a helicopter is on the left side. Peter climbed into the pilot's seat and rolled his left leg over the yoke, which in a chopper really isn't a yoke at all, but a cyclic. In layman's terms, it's the joystick that allows a chopper to move forward, backwards, and sideways.

He looked at me and said, "Don't touch anything."

"That goes without saying," I thought as I surveyed the vast array of avionics. When I looked down, I immediately noticed the floor was actually clear Plexiglas. I found this quite unsettling.

There is something unique about being inside a chopper during the startup sequence. The pilot switches on the battery, and his instrument panel bounces to life. The engine sputters and then churns. Then the unmistakable whiz of the turbine fills the air as the manifold pressure builds, and the rotor begins to turn ever so slowly. A few moments later, the engine is roaring, and you are ready for takeoff.

Takeoff was as smooth as silk. I felt as if I were the king of the world as Chopper 7 ascended, moving slowly forward about ten feet above the ground, until the control tower gave us the "all clear." We wore noise-canceling headphones to talk with one another. Peter explained that I should watch for and alert him to all air traffic I observed. I felt like an old pro when I informed him, "You've got a light plane at eleven o'clock."

As we climbed up and into Denver's Front Range, I was amazed by how many people had swimming pools. It felt glorious as we flew into the Rocky Mountains. A herd of deer took notice below.

As we neared the end of our flight, the terrain turned mountainous and semi-barren. We were above the tree line, a harsh place where climate and altitude make the environment inhospitable to trees. I noticed we were flying low, perhaps less than 100 feet from the ground. Suddenly, our air speed slowed as Peter began to creep forward. Then he began to hover. We were at the peak of the Continental Divide, less than fifty feet from a rocky cliff and roughly twenty-five feet off the ground. After several minutes, I asked Peter, "Why are we hovering?"

"Well, I underestimated our weight," he squawked in his charming Aussie accent. "We don't have enough thrust to get over, and not enough fuel to get home." His voice was calm, as if he'd done this a million times.

I thought, "What kind of madman flies an overweight chopper through the Rockies?" I suppose I began to become concerned for our wellbeing. "How he could put our lives at risk? Reckless…. He's going to get us killed," I thought.

"So what do we do?" I asked, fully expecting we would have to crash land and wait for rescue if we survived.

"I'm waiting for an updraft," he said as he carefully surveyed the terrain around us. Several minutes later, he inched the chopper closer toward the rocky face and inched upwards. We cleared the face by a dozen feet. We popped over the

Continental Divide to the breathtaking sight of Vail Valley below.

It was smooth sailing from that point. Our landing was seamless. My fear quickly subsided. For the first time in my life, I felt I had achieved celebrity status. The eyes of the ultra-rich jet set were on our jet ranger as we touched down.

As a cycling enthusiast, I was anxious to prove myself in the field and went about the job of getting the story. But deep within, I was still confused and could not help but wonder how the hell we were going to make it home.

Thankfully, just before our return to Denver, Peter explained that the updraft was in our favor on this side of the mountain range. Indeed, the evening thermals allowed the craft to climb effortlessly up and over the divide.

The following day, I was up early and off to the airfield for the next stage of the international bicycle race. Our destination was Aspen. The famous resort was served by an airline that locals referred to as Aspen "Scareways," aptly nicknamed because of the airport runway's proximity to the mountains and the rollercoaster effect of take-offs and landings.

To my great surprise, the trip into Aspen was uneventful. In fact, my jitters about flying with Peter all but faded away after he reassured us in his easy manner about better managing his ballast. Going home, however, was an entirely different matter. Our trip home in Chopper 7 started as smooth as a whistle. We were flying fast and fairly low to the ground. As we approached a mountain ridge, Peter suddenly announced, "God make us truly grateful for what we are about to receive."

As we crossed over the ridge, Chopper 7 shook violently. It sounded like the rotors actually slowed as a strong wind gust pushed us downward. I was mortified. This scenario was repeated at every ridge crossing. For the first time, Peter did not look like his usual relaxed self. It was more of a look of, "I think we may be in trouble here, boys." It was the most difficult flight I've ever taken. It was impossible to write my story about the bike race in flight. Worse, I never wanted to fly in a helicopter again.

Such is not the fate of a sports reporter in Colorado, and so I was tasked to cover Wyoming football. Reluctant to board Chopper 7 again, I was indifferent about finding the backup pilot on duty. He brought along a friend, who happened to be another chopper pilot. After 130 miles or so as the crow flies, it was clear that our trip to Laramie was nothing like going to the Rockies. The terrain below was perfectly flat. In the event of an emergency, I thought, we could put down virtually anywhere.

Landing at War Memorial Stadium was unreal. I mean, how many people get to land at a football game in the parking lot? It was awesome, and I felt like a rock star. Better yet, I felt relaxed. But apparently the story of our Aspen adventure got back to these pilots, so on our return trip, they decided to have a little fun at my expense.

We were floating smoothly over the Great Plains when Chopper 7 suddenly dropped and began to fall to earth. It was my first lesson on auto rotation. The pilot had disengaged the rotors to joust me for a ready laugh. From my reaction, it worked. In fact, it worked three more times on our trip home from Laramie.

"What a bunch of yahoos," I thought to myself. "Man, how can they be so reckless?" I no longer felt safe in choppers.

Worse than that, I had a strong premonition, a "knowing." Someone was going to die.

I'd planned to write about this for many years, and when I finally put pen to paper (so to speak) to spin this tale of reckless flying, I was deeply saddened, yet not surprised to learn that Peter Peelgrane had been critically injured when he was forced to auto-rotate his helicopter into the frozen waters of Horsetooth Reservoir. According to reports, Peter, then employed by KUSA 9 Denver, was flying in a thick fog over the reservoir, west of Fort Collins, when the engine failed. He slowed the fall with auto-rotation, and was able to crash land on an ice flow.

Peter had two passengers aboard. Both were freelance photographers, and both were his friends. Peter watched helplessly as one, and then the other, slid beneath the surface. When rescuers finally reached Peter, he was clinically dead. His core body temperature was 72 degrees, as low as has been recorded among hypothermia survivors. Yes, I said survivors. Peter was transported to a Fort Collins hospital, where doctors warmed him, opened his chest, and then restarted his heart.

Peelgrane died three years later from brain injuries suffered during the crash. He was only forty-nine.

CHAPTER 25

PEAK 13

I was once an expert skier. I did road reports in the Rocky Mountains for Metro Traffic in Denver, which made me very popular with area ski resorts. I found that many times it would snow in Denver, yet be clear as a bell in the mountains. Since the media reported from the city, they tended to put their focus there. Mine was the voice that told them if they were able to climb above, say, Georgetown, they would be greeted by sunshine, dry roads, and A-plus ski conditions. My reports brought thousands of people to the slopes who would have stayed home fearing that snow in Denver meant a blizzard in the high country.

I'd spend my weekend mornings enlightening Denverites, and then carve up some unsuspecting slope in a session of ski mountain madness in Summit County, Colorado. I was based out of the Loveland Basin ski resort. Until I arrived, Loveland was the best-kept secret around. It is on the Denver side (east) of the Continental Divide at the Eisenhower tunnel. Now, what most people don't know is storms often stall at this very spot as they generate energy to try to push over the divide. When that occurs, Loveland receives much more snow than its neighboring competitors. At least that is what Loveland Basin's general manager, Otto Werlin, explained to me.

Werlin was an older man who stood almost 6'7". Resort employees often joked that I was his "negative son" (a clever reference to me being black) because he seemed to dote over me so. My reports clearly generated extra revenue, and Otto was most appreciative. Otto asked early on whether I wanted to learn to ski.

"Sure," I said. "But I don't think you are gonna have ski boots in my size."

Otto gave me a big smile. "Wanna bet?" he said with a wink.

Werlin was a Sasquatch advocate. He took it upon himself to make sure anyone with a big foot could have an opportunity to ski. Sure enough, his rental shop presented me with an extra-large San Marco Boot that fit my foot snug as a bug. Otto sent me out for private lessons with his best instructor, and I've been carving mountains ever since.

Honestly, I find it amusing when experts chat with you on a ski lift. Then toward the end, they ask you to make a run down the mountain with them, fully knowing their intention is to turn and burn down the slopes as you are left atop the mountain to admire what wonderful skiers they are. I love the expression on their faces as they turn, expecting to see me fumbling and stumbling to get down that double black diamond. Hot on their heels, these are the times I love to hockey stop, tossing just enough snow into their faces so it doesn't look intentional. No one expects a giant black man to be able to ski, let alone at expert status.

I love to tell the story of the kids from the Loveland Basin ski team who took a liking to me. They begged me to make some runs with them after my shift. It was an offer I could not refuse. I followed as closely as I could as they darted through the trees on trails I never knew existed. Suddenly, they vanished before my eyes. My first impulse was to ski faster to try to catch up, but my instinct told me to hit the brakes, which I did—at the edge of a twenty-foot drop-off.

The kids, a boy and a girl, were waiting below with big smiles on their faces.

"JUMP! JUMP! Your skis will land flat," they shouted, in an attempt to egg me on. Cornered like a frightened cat, I surveyed the terrain below. We were beyond the boundaries of the ski area, and this was the only way back. "JUMP! JUMP! Your skis will land flat!"

And you know what? They did. After hitting the ground with such force, I struggled to stand, forcing my legs to move me up. I almost made it, but eventually came to rest on my butt. Kids!

In December 1985, I couldn't wait to make fresh tracks on a brand-new area of Keystone Resort. The largest ski area in Summit County, Colorado had recently expanded its north peak. It was named Peak 13.

When I finally hit the slopes, a sense of foreboding came over me. I was surprised to find the area had lots of icy patches that diminished the experience. But I couldn't shake the feeling that something was not right.

On only our second run, as we were on the lift, I turned to a friend I was skiing with and said, "Let's get out of here. This place is death."

I wasn't sure why I felt such trepidation, or why I was moved to describe this back bowl in such a morbid way. But my friend agreed, and we left that side of the mountain, never to return. When my friends in Denver asked me about my experience at the new area, I found myself repeating the same term I'd said on the lift chair. "Avoid that place; it's death."

There was no mention of conditions like the icy terrain or black versus blue diamonds, simply my dreadful feeling about the place.

Sometime later, I learned the giant wheel that operates the lift dropped from its encasement, causing a major bullwhip-like ripple down the cable that holds lift chairs. There were hundreds of people on the lift. Many were catapulted forty feet into the air. Some were impaled on trees. Fifty people were seriously injured. Two lost their lives.

It took me thirty years to admit to being a bit of a psychic. Sometimes it's little things. Sometimes not. Perhaps the ability to glimpse the future is a means of self-preservation, like the sixth sense animals possess prior to an earthquake. It could not be causation since I could not sense impending doom for others. I personally felt danger. I'm sure I'm not the only one who has had these experiences, which inevitably brings me to the question "Why?" As in, "Why me?"

So far, the only answer I've gotten is, "Why not?"

CHAPTER 26

REASONING WITH REASONER

After bidding farewell to Denver for the second time, I traveled to the family homestead in Coconut Grove, Florida. I was able to find a job as a television reporter at a local station, but the news director could not give me a start date. Seems there was a hiring freeze because the network affiliates in Miami were about to flip-flop.

My resources were depleted, and I would have been homeless. Luckily, my great-grandfather Stirrup had a provision in his will that any family member in need could stay in the home he built. I sent a flood of resumes to the hippest companies I could think of. Imagine my surprise when I received a call from Miller Brewing Company, offering to fly me to Milwaukee to interview for a job in their public relations department. I'd never done PR, and I had no idea what it entailed, but I was willing to try.

The morning of my interview, I went to the hotel restaurant for breakfast. There was an old man sitting at the counter who had just finished his breakfast. He looked a bit disheveled. After studying his bill circumspectly, he pulled out his change purse. I laughed inside as he gazed into the purse through the bottom of his spectacles. He carefully laid a few coins on the counter as the tip. Upon closer examination, I realized it was Harry Reasoner of CBS News. I immediately got up and introduced myself to him.

PAUL DEAN JACKSON

I have a great affection for old-school broadcasters, particularly Reasoner. I loved his work on *60 Minutes* and was a big fan of his writing. I think I may have mentioned I wasn't a big reader, and usually only read what I liked. Reasoner made me feel as if that was normal, writing in his memoir *Before the Colors Fade*:

> If there is one rule I would recommend to any reader not specifically engaged in studying for an examination, it would be to read only what you like. It doesn't matter what it is: if you don't like it, don't read it. Reading is a pleasure or it is nothing.... Reading is about the only thing left in life that should be preserved for pure pleasure.

His observation obviously struck a chord with me. I never returned his book to the San Pedro branch library, where I'd borrowed it so many years ago. My mother (the head librarian) eventually told me to keep it.

"Mr. Reasoner," I explained, "I'm a television journalist, but I'm having trouble finding work. I'm here for an interview with Miller Brewing."

Instead of wishing me luck, he asked, "Do you love television news?"

I answered in the affirmative.

"Well, if that's what you love, that's what you should do." He offered no other words. No pearls of how to get back in the business, other than telling me that I should. I shook his hand, thanked him, and he left.

During the entire interview process for Miller Brewing Company, all I could think about was my conversation with Harry Reasoner and how exciting it was to meet him. I wasn't fully concentrating on the interview. Instead, I was focused on what he'd said. Stay the course and try to regain a foothold in television news. This major distraction probably kept me from being fully present during the interview. That, in combination with my horrible spelling skills (there was no auto-correct back then), likely prevented me from nailing a lucrative career with Miller since it was looking for minority candidates.

CHAPTER 27

I AM HERE

At one time or another, most of us have wondered about what happens after we die. Do our bodies simply decompose and return to nature as soil? Or does the essence of what we once were (our spirit or consciousness, if you will) live on in the invisible realm? I prefer to believe the latter. Not for peace of mind or because my Christian upbringing promised that if we lead good lives, then we'll be rewarded by eternal life in heaven. I believe it because of numerous experiences throughout my life that cannot be explained.

I was raised in a matriarchal household. My grandmother, Kate Stirrup Dean, inherited the keys to the kingdom from her father, who amassed enormous wealth as he pioneered South Florida. When she passed away at the age of ninety, all were present at her funeral as glorious words of love and affection were spoken in her memory.

At least that's what I'd like to believe. The truth is that I did not attend my grandmother's funeral. My mother was stricken with grief upon hearing of her death, so she instructed my older sister, Elizabeth, to relay the heartbreaking news to me.

I remember feeling lonely one day, so I called home to talk to my mother. It was good to hear her voice, and we had a long, pleasant conversation. Before we said our goodbyes, I inquired about my grandmother.

"Paul," she said in an angry voice. "You know Grandma Dean is dead."

I was stunned. No one had told me that my grandmother, the woman I loved so much, had been gone for months. She had passed, and no one had so much as whispered a word to me, let alone wondered why I did not attend the funeral.

It was beyond my understanding at the time why anyone would intentionally engage in such a sinister act.

Growing up, Elizabeth did mean things like making up songs about me. Her best was a catchy tune, with an upbeat celebratory tone. "You're gonna die in Vietnam. You're gonna die in Vietnam." Luckily for me, at eighteen, I was too tall for the draft.

I believe my grandmother knew of the affront. And so, some years later, an invisible force called me to her grave. I was living in my great-grandfather's house in Miami at the time, searching for a job in TV news. Money was short, and times were hard.

One night, my cousin Gary invited me out to party with him. One drink led to another, which led to another, and by the end of the evening, I was drunk off my ass. The region was new to me, Gary was driving, and I had no idea where we were.

Suddenly, a voice in my head said quietly, "I'm here." I rose from my slumped position in the front seat, straightened my back, and stretched erect, much like an animal in the wild listening for a sound in the distance.

"I'm here," said the voice.

"Where's Grandma buried?" I asked my cousin.

He laughed and turned to look at me. "Funny you would ask that," he said. "We just passed the graveyard." Apparently thinking it might be fun to wander the graveyard in our drunken state, Gary asked, "Do you want to see her grave?"

I nodded, and he quickly turned the car around and drove to the family cemetery just two blocks away. It was pitch black as we stumbled out of the car and entered the cemetery. Gary, still laughing and in a jovial mood from a night of heavy drinking, informed me, "She's buried over here."

I'd never set foot in the graveyard, so I paused, turned to Gary, and said, "No…. She's here." I walked in the darkness, drawn by an invisible force. I crisscrossed gravestones and respectfully stepped over gravesites. I finally stopped at the foot of one of the graves. Without even reading the headstone, I lifted my head and emerged from my trance-like state, quietly standing in front of her grave.

"Here she is."

I finally looked down to confirm what I already knew and read her headstone. I began to sob uncontrollably. My grandmother had reached out through time and space to lead me there. The experience superseded all affronts from my absence at her funeral.

When I was a child, she used to say, "Where's my boy?"

It is out of the ordinary for me, and as a broadcaster, I can only relay this story in print. I've tried on many occasions to speak it aloud, but before I can complete it, I am overwhelmed with emotion as if the events were unfolding before me in real-time, and I find myself sobbing and unable to speak. Grandmother Dean, whom I loved so dearly, had reached out from the grave to tell me she loved me, and all was well.

Following that experience, I often sat in silence hoping to hear the voice in my head once again say, "I am here," but there is only silence. But sometimes, just sometimes, the silence responds, "I AM."

CHAPTER 28

STRUCK BY LIGHTNING

I am deathly afraid of lightning. At the first sign of electrical activity, I am the first to run for shelter. My trepidation comes through firsthand experience, but that was not always the case. As a rookie sports reporter at KMGH television, I was sent to cover the PGA Senior Tour in Castle Rock, Colorado. It was a long, hard day of work tracking golf's elite and grabbing interviews. But by afternoon, I was prepared and anxious for my five o'clock live shot. Just as the newscast began, a torrential rainstorm swept into the area. By the time the sports segment rolled around, I stood soaking wet in the middle of the golf course. Lightning lit up the sky around me. The wonderful on-camera introduction I had worked so hard to create was now an illegible running mass of ink.

Now, at one time or another, you have probably seen TV news vans (or "live trucks," as we call them in the business) on the road. That thing on the top that looks like a large radar dish is actually a telescoping antenna that extends high into the air in order to send microwaves or broadcast signals back to the television station.

Scientists say the odds of an average person living in the U.S. being struck by lightning in a given year are one in 700,000. I am pretty certain those statistics do not include people standing next to a lightning rod or, in this case, a few feet away from a live truck with the mast fully extended.

PAUL DEAN JACKSON

Perhaps the odds were in our favor, or maybe providence shone down on us that day. In any event, our lightning magnet never caught a bolt, and I managed to survive that ill-advised live shot.

Speaking of lightning, I'll bet you had no idea Florida is the lightning capital of the United States. And that's exactly where I was one fateful afternoon with my cousin's ex-wife Diane and her five-year-old son, George.

Diane invited me to tag along with them on a trip to the beach. The beautiful day of soaking in the hot waters of Biscayne Bay soon gave way to cloudy skies. In the distance, you could see a storm rolling in. Little George was having a wonderful time, and we paid little attention as the crowded beach began to thin. Soon after we saw lightning on the horizon, Diane said, "Okay, George; it's time to go." Of course, the little boy operated on his own schedule and paid no attention. Soon after, the sky began to grow black and we could hear the thunder and see the lightning. "Georgie, it's time to go," his mother insisted, but little George paid no attention.

As I gathered my things and waited for Diane to gather up her little boy, I noticed we were the only ones left on the beach. The storm was almost over us.

"Come on, George. *It's time to go!*" she shouted, but little George would not listen.

"Diane," I said. "We've got to get out of here."

Then, in her sternest voice, she commanded her son to come, but the little boy (spoiled, to say the least) was not used to taking orders from his mother, and he definitely would not start on this day. The storm was directly overhead as Diane finally took action. She picked him up, and said, "George, we are going *now*!"

At that moment, I heard a loud explosion overhead and dove to the ground. In midair, I felt a jab on the top of my head. It felt as if someone had taken a pickax and, instead of completing the down stroke and fracturing my skull, pulled back at the last moment, delivering a hard prick. The force of the event drove me hard into the sand. "Have I been struck by lightning?" I wondered through my haze. "No, that couldn't have happened. I'm still alive."

Thoroughly disgusted that I'd allowed myself to be put in this kind of danger, I left George and his mother on the beach. I searched for any shelter I could find. Obviously, not thinking clearly, and not wanting to be exposed to rain or the sky above, I huddled under a tall tree. A few minutes later, little George popped into view and ran over to join me. His mother was close behind and finally showed a bit of intestinal fortitude by screaming at the top of her lungs, "George! Get away from that tree!" And this time, he actually listened.

The next day, Diane asked me to come by her house. She wanted to show me something. "Look at the burn marks on the beach blanket," she said. "You really were struck by lightning." There it was: proof I'd been struck by lightning and—lived to tell the tale. I felt no ill effects, but soon after, that spot on my skull turned soft and remained that way for many years.

In my estimation, a small residual bolt from a nearby ground strike hit me. At 6'10" and the tallest thing on the beach, I'm sure that if I hadn't dived to the ground, I would be dead. Instead, I walked away.

PAUL DEAN JACKSON

When I saw Diane again years later, she was quick to mention how I left them on the beach. I just smiled and said, "Yep, I sure did." Then, I thought quietly, "And I would leave you again, but next time much sooner."

CHAPTER 29

I SEE GOD IN YOU

I could hardly contain my awe as I entered the famous Crystal Cathedral. It was, after all, the second-most famous attraction in Orange County, California, after Disneyland. I was on assignment with the Orange County News Channel, checking in on the health and welfare of popular televangelist and motivational speaker Robert H. Schuller, following his miraculous recovery from two brain surgeries.

After what he described as a light bump on the head while getting into a car in the Netherlands, his injury escalated from a slight headache to a traumatic brain injury overnight. I'd readily volunteered for the assignment. I'd heard about Rev. Schuller long before the cathedral was even a thought. My high school girlfriend's family was part of the congregation that gathered in a drive-in movie theater parking lot to hear his sermons. She encouraged me to come listen to her preacher, but back then, crossing over the so-called Orange curtain meant crossing the color line. Local police jurisdictions made it clear that African-Americans were not welcome in the OC, so I never chanced the trip.

Designed by award-winning architect Philip Johnson, the Crystal Cathedral has the notoriety of being the first-ever, all-glass church. It is undoubtedly one of the most beautiful structures in Southern California. I am quite sure I looked like a precocious grade-schooler with my eyes affixed to the shimmering glass above. I wondered aloud, "How much effort does it take to keep ten-thousand windows virtually spotless?"

Over the years, I had come to admire Robert Schuller's lectures on the power of positive thinking, or "Possibility Thinking," as he called it. I owned and frequently listened to his cassettes, feeding my mind with positive messages and affirmations to elevate my mental state.

"Grab hold of a rope. A rope called hope, and then you can cope!" he would proclaim.

When Robert Schuller entered the Crystal Cathedral, I was amazed to see that he appeared to be in perfect health. There was no shaven head, no signs of trauma or surgeries. He was able to walk with no assistance, and he approached me with an obvious zest for life and a broad smile.

"This is Paul Jackson from the Orange County News Channel," his assistant said.

Rev. Schuller leaned his head back and, with a whimsical look of admiration, examined me closely through his thick eyeglasses.

"I see God in you," were the first words from his mouth.

Ordinarily, I would have been floored by this observation, especially coming from the sage who offered hope to so many, but Dr. Schuller's words harkened back to an echo lodged in the depths of my mind.

In Tulsa, Oklahoma, my eyes were fixed on Oral Roberts as he approached me, straight out of his prayer tower. I was the new television sports reporter in town. I was Tulsa's first

African American sports anchor, which the local paper heavily publicized at the time.

If you don't know, Oral Roberts was the first evangelist to lead large televised revivals in which worshipers claimed to be miraculously healed. His fame grew with the 1965 opening of Oral Roberts University in Tulsa. By 1969, he was America's second best-known televangelist, behind his friend Billy Graham. Roberts spoke of divine visions and messages from God throughout his life. This sometimes brought public ridicule, such as his reported 1980 encounter with a 900-foot-tall Jesus. In 1987, he claimed that God told him he would die if a fundraising goal were not met. As I recall, Roberts sat atop his prayer tower in the middle of the ORU campus for weeks, until a million dollars materialized through various donations.

I felt as if Roberts might have been in the rapture of another divine vision as he approached me with his son Richard, courtside in the campus sports complex. I was there to cover a men's basketball game. After a polite introduction from Richard, Oral Roberts paused as if he were sizing me up. He looked up at me, deep into my eyes, then leaned in close as if to let me in on a secret..."I see God in you," he proclaimed to me on a very personal level. The statement was unexpected. As his son looked on with a full smile, I was floored to the point of near paralysis by his observation.

I have searched for God for most of my life, imploring Him to appear before me and prove His existence. Growing up in the Episcopal Church, I assumed God was a man who'd dwelled in the sky above, looking down to shepherd the people He created.

The closest I came to proof of His existence occurred one morning at Camp Bishop Stevens in Julian, California. I attended Camp Stevens every summer, enjoying swimming, arts and crafts, and friendship in the great outdoors. Religion was a small part of the program, although I don't recall enjoying attending the outdoor services. Really, who wants to go to church when you can be swimming or hiking? The services were held in a quiet corner of the camp that housed a beautiful wooden outdoor altar and pews made from fallen trees. As I sat in this beautiful place, listening but not hearing the service, something moved me inside. There were no words, simply grace, peace, and the feeling something much greater than me was soothing me with its presence. It was such a pleasurable experience that once the service was over and the campers moved on to other activities, I remained behind to sit quietly in prayer. When I thought everyone was gone, I scanned the area, waiting for God to appear before me. I knew He was there and talking to me. At that moment, I noticed three other campers were still there. We looked at one another for a while without words and then came together in a circle.

"Did you feel that?" one of the campers asked.

I assumed God had only communicated with me. In fact, He'd spoken to everyone present, and He was offering proof of divine contact through commonality. Of the dozens of people present, only four of us were receptive enough to hear the un-hearable. The experience was so powerful that we all began to cry. Then we left, hand in hand, knowing we'd just had a conversation with God.

I returned to that spot often. Year after year, I sat in front of the chapel in quiet contemplation, thinking this was the place God dwelled, or at least a conduit that allowed Him to appear. But never again did I experience such a holy moment there.

As I stated earlier, my personal views on religion changed in college. I decided God was not a person, but a construct. Since "God" is called by different names throughout the world, I decided to use the words "The Force" instead of God. I felt evolved telling people, "May the Force be with you." Oddly enough, I think most who received my greeting instantly knew my meaning.

As my understanding of science and the world expanded, I began to realize that my definition of God as a Force was the closest I would ever come to the truth about Its existence. I was drawn to the New Thought spiritual movement, which was not afraid to use science to better identify the God presence. My desire to learn placed Spiritual teachers on my path. But none taught me more than a young black man with a squeaky voice, preaching in a warehouse in Santa Monica. When the preacher opened his mouth, all I heard was a young kid screaming at the congregation. Apparently, he hadn't come prepared with a sermon and seemed to be spouting off random thoughts. Finally, he confessed to the congregation that he was still waiting. Suddenly, he began to speak in a smooth and fluid tone. He described the roots of metaphysics and philosophy as if words were being channeled through him from a higher source, eventually explaining (at least to me) the fundamental nature of being.

It was clear to me this young preacher was connected to a higher source. The young teacher taught me the importance of affirmative prayer, engaging my mind in creating the change I wish to see in my life. He based his philosophy around the teaching of the Religious Science movement. Its founder, Ernest Holmes, taught that through the power of our minds, we are continually creating the conditions of our life. He believed that the thoughts, attitudes, and beliefs we hold are shaping our tomorrows. In essence, thoughts are things, or as I like to say, "Act as though you are, and you will be."

I stayed connected with this young preacher as his church, the Agape International Spiritual Center, and his congregation grew, and his voice lowered with maturity. Word of his remarkable connection to spirit spread, and suddenly, young Dr. Michael Bernard Beckwith, whom I considered my friend, began to take on celebrity status, appearing on *The Oprah Winfrey Show* and in the movie *The Secret* to explain the existence of the God Force.

If I were, however, to recommend a movie about the topic, it would not be *The Secret*, but *What the Bleep Do We Know!?* To the uninitiated, the content is simply mind-blowing. It contends that the universe is not constructed from matter, but from thought, and that everything, even God, is energy. Energy, after all, can neither be created nor destroyed. And like God, it always has been and always will be. It has the ability to go into form and out of form. Therefore, God, like energy, is indeed within us and without us.

What the Bleep Do We Know!? introduced me to innovative science on the atom, which I grew up believing was solid matter. We now know that even the smallest part of an atom, the nucleus, is simply a probability cloud that pops in and out of existence and, therefore, is not solid at all. Quantum mechanics, therefore, proves there is no separation between God and us. In fact, we are all connected by an invisible strand we call energy.

Finally, I was able to make sense of what Rev. Schuller and Oral Roberts meant when each said, "I see God in you."

Perhaps philosopher Ernest Holmes best expressed it in the early 1940s:

> How can we expect to realize God in the emptiness of
> space if we have refused to see God in those we meet?
> And how can we find God in those we meet in the events

that transpire around us unless we have first discovered God at the center of our own being? We cannot.

The starting point is at the center of our own being. When we awaken to the Divine within us, it will reach out and embrace everything around us, and it will discover the same Presence in people, in events, and in all nature. For God is not separate from what he is doing. The Divine life is in everyone and in everything.

— *365 Science of Mind: A Year of Daily Wisdom from Ernest Holmes*

Obviously, this is my definition of God through science...what many call source energy, the great "I Am." That same energy directed me to write this memoir. But while it wishes to express itself through me, the eternal answer remains one for the great philosophers of our time.

"I Am." Is it a response from God? Or my ego? I am without an answer.

CHAPTER 30

PARANORMAL

When it comes to paranormal activity, I am not a brave man.

"There's no such thing as ghost...there's no such thing as ghost." As a child, I repeated that phrase in my mind anytime I was afraid, mostly of the dark. But after an experience in Philadelphia, I can never repeat that statement definitively for comfort.

We had just arrived in the City of Brotherly Love. My new station, NBC-10, set my family up in temporary housing near the station while we settled in and searched for a permanent home. Our accommodations were lovely, a furnished two-bedroom apartment in the Overbrook section of the city known as the Executive House.

As the newest reporter on staff, I never knew what my schedule would be from day to day. And so it was I drew the morning news shift one week. I awoke before sunrise, feeling wide-awake and rearing to go as I rode the elevator down to the parking level. When the door opened, I peeked out cautiously. Being new to the city, I wasn't about to let my guard down for potential muggers. Standing tall, I was ready for anything. I was pleasantly surprised to find I was not the only person up at such an ungodly hour. To my right, perhaps thirty yards away, I saw a woman standing at the edge of the parking structure, looking down at something. I assumed she was searching for the keys to the car next to her.

I remember thinking, "Wow! I'm not alone. It's silly of me to worry about muggers in this complex." Since it was still dark, my concern turned to the woman. I wondered whether I might freak her out, being a huge black man.

Still, I was exceedingly happy to see another person at that hour. As the elevator door closed behind me, I rattled my keys to alert her of my presence and walked toward my SUV. I observed the woman carefully, prepared to give her a friendly good morning greeting, when our eyes met. I passed in front of a support beam no more than a foot wide, and in that instance—no more than a fraction of a second—she disappeared.

I visually checked where she'd been standing. Then I scanned the garage, checking the area three times. There was no one to be found. I was completely alone in the parking structure. Whoever, or whatever, it was had literally vanished.

This, for lack of a better term, freaked me out.

When I climbed into my truck, I was terrified. I feared a dark presence, and I had to muster every ounce of my courage just to lift my eyes and gaze into the rearview mirror to back out of my space. I feared some sort of ungodly entity would suddenly pop into view, as often happens in horror movies.

The mystery rattled my brain so much that I only spoke of the incident to my wife. The inexplicability of the woman's sudden disappearance led me to believe there was a real possibility I'd encountered a poltergeist. And in that instant, I went from fears to tears, wondering why it had to be me who experienced such an unsettling event.

I never faced my fears; instead, I left my truck parked on the street for the remainder of our time at the Executive House. Every morning, I'd wonder, "Why me? Why did I have to experience that vanishing act?"

Sometime later, I told my previously unspoken story to my good friend Ellen Steinberg, who was attending a conference in Philadelphia. Ellen is a self-professed psychic I met in Denver. She was a guest on a late-night talk program on KOA Radio, where I was a weekend news anchor. Once off the air, I approached her, thinking it would be entertaining to get a "psychic reading." I suppose it was written in the stars that we would be friends as we instantly clicked and became as close as family.

After listening to me tell my ghost story, Ellen immediately spoke. "Why did you think she was looking for keys?" she quizzed.

I could not answer. In fact, it was simply my assumption. I'd never actually seen keys. When I replayed that morning in my mind, all I saw was a woman standing at the edge of the garage looking down to her side.

"It is interesting you thought she was searching for keys. There is a message for you in that," my friend concluded.

"Yes! Finding the key," I thought. This simple observation struck me as colossal. But it opened a wormhole I did not care to enter. I left our conversation there. Let sleeping ghosts lie, I thought. I have never since had another paranormal encounter like that, nor do I care to.

I remembered the encounter years later, while spending an evening with a medicine woman from the Shift Center in Garden City, Kansas. One of my dearest friends, Everard Hughes, who happened to be a long-time neighbor from

Southern California, owned the facility. Everard was an oncologist, and his wife, Chris, ran the Shift Center for cancer survivors. Chris thought I might benefit from undergoing transformative therapy called E.F.T., or the Emotional Freedom Technique for some life issues that were gnawing at me.

While my session was underway, the medicine woman (who was not Native American but claimed to be a psychic healer) paused suddenly and began scanning the ceiling with her eyes. After a few minutes, she turned toward me abruptly, asking, "Who is Phyllis?"

"Huh?" I uttered.

"Do you have a relative named Phyllis?"

I did not. She told me that a female entity named Phyllis was in the room and had taken a keen interest in me. She described her as a tall redhead who stood straight, was very stern, and seemed to be extremely possessive of me.

Well into our session, which I later learned went well beyond traditional E.F.T. techniques, I apparently hit an emotional block, releasing past hurt and pain. The medicine woman claimed the entity helped her pinpoint my psychic injury, then aided in removing this deep-rooted pain, which she says was replaced with love energy. Phyllis then, apparently, left the building.

I can't claim a miraculous healing, nor do I even know the true result of my session if any. I do know I listened intently throughout and was open to all possibilities. I also know I slept like a rock and awoke feeling refreshed.

"Could Phyllis have appeared before me in the parking garage in Philadelphia?" I later wondered. If so, then what is the key?

My most recent knowing was in April 2014. I had a waking dream of a giant fireball entering the Earth's atmosphere and flying over my house. I waited for the blast from impact. I fully expected a catastrophic explosion, but it never came.

When I awoke from my dream, I learned a meteor had hit Russia, blowing out windows and injuring more than a thousand people. I was amazed but not surprised when I saw dash cam videos from the northwest Russian city of Murmansk. The meteorite burning up in the atmosphere was the exact image I saw in my dream.

CHAPTER 31

L.A. RIOTS

On April 29, 1992, I was partying like a madman on Santa Catalina Island. A few days earlier, I'd been fired from my job at the Orange County News Channel, the region's first local twenty-four-hour cable news operation, where I served as weekend anchor and reporter. The circumstances surrounding my release were egregious; a single phone call from my attorney yielded an outcome that was most desirable, at least to me. I was one of the channel's earliest hires, compiling reports long before the inaugural broadcast. I left my indelible imprint on OCN through memorable features and electrifying live shots.

One of my many stories had to do with Elvira Jordan, a woman who agreed to be a surrogate mother, but changed her mind during pregnancy, and went to court to keep the baby. The case spawned a media frenzy led by OCN, which covered the proceedings like a soap opera. Jordan's attorney, Richard Thomas, would gain national fame from the trial.

Our acting news director did not think highly of Thomas or Jordan, insinuating they were in it for the publicity and money. Since I was the father of a lost child, I found the legal repercussions surrounding this case utterly fascinating. The interviews I conducted with Thomas were long and exhaustive. It took a great deal of effort to sift through the trivial and find the meat of the issue. Over the course of the trial, I became his most trusted conduit of information. In fact, an exclusive, surreptitious recording of a conversation between Jordan and the biological father led to my termination.

Thomas felt personally responsible for my dismissal. Knowing there was no wrongdoing on my part, he offered his legal representation. And I accepted. A single phone call yielded a document that precludes me from discussing the matter further.

Let's just say as my birthday gift to myself, I paid off my car loan in cash, and other than finding a new job, I didn't have a care in the world.

I was dating a smoking hot stockbroker, who had just tucked my inebriated butt into bed at my apartment in Huntington Beach. After giving me a final birthday kiss, she set off to her beautiful estate on Lookout Mountain, high above Laurel Canyon, rockin' down the highway, with the top down in her bright red Corvette.

I woke up from my daze at midnight and realized she'd left. For whatever reason, I decided to switch on the television. L.A. was burning. I was mortified; I was certain my girlfriend had been carjacked and was probably dead. I immediately called her. I was relieved to hear her smooth German accent, which gave way to a crackle in her voice. She had just arrived home after negotiating numerous detours and riot zones.

I watched the coverage in disbelief, feeling totally displaced. That morning, I drove to Carson to check on my mother.

It was surreal to see the number of gunmen on rooftops, presumably to protect their businesses. I could see plumes of smoke from building fires on the horizon. At that moment, I needed to get back into the news game in the worst possible way.

Tormented is the only way I can adequately describe the way I felt when I viewed the now-infamous attack on truck driver Reginald Denny, who happened to be in the wrong place at the wrong time. "The person doing this has crossed the line," I thought. "If I were there, reporting from the scene, I would have stepped in and stopped him."

It was beyond my understanding how someone could be brutally attacked on live TV without a police response. When his attacker slammed a brick into Denny's skull and raised his arms in triumph, I'd seen enough.

I called Warren Carringeno, the news director at KTLA, and asked him for an opportunity to report. It was not the first time I'd met Carringeno. I had been trying on a tie at Nordstrom's in Orange County (wondering whether I could afford it) when a stranger walked up to me.

"Nice tie," he said, matter-of-factly.

"It is a *beautiful* tie," I thought to myself.

After introducing himself as the news director of KTLA, he shocked me by saying he knew who I was, and that he was a fan of my work at OCN. I instantly had a "knowing" that our paths would cross again. Oh yes, and I bought the tie.

The timing of my call could not have been better since many reporters in Los Angeles preferred to avoid the uprising, which would claim more than fifty lives. Hell, they were scared. This was my chance.

Warren asked me to report to duty the following morning.

I don't recall signing paperwork, just being escorted to the assignment desk for a brief introduction. Someone gave me a bulletproof vest and told me to head to Compton for a ride-along with the first Marine Expeditionary Force out of Camp Pendleton. Their mission was to sit atop the powder keg known as South Central Los Angeles and enforce a dusk to dawn curfew.

I could begin by telling you about the amazing amount of weaponry the boys in green were packing. But the first and most vivid memory of my coverage of the L.A. riots is Geraldo Rivera. He and his network crew arrived late for the ride-along and delayed our departure as he bantered with the commander after a Marine informed him the troop carrier was full.

Rivera smiled, scanned the vehicle, and looked directly at me. "Bump them," he said. He was requesting KTLA, and the reporter no one had ever seen, be bumped to make the space available to a network news reporter.

The Marine doubled-checked the roster. "I have KTLA on the list, sir," he told Rivera. "*You* are not on the list," he added.

Rivera had a look of utter shock and disbelief as the convoy pulled away without him. "What an asshole," I thought. Some other reporters actually said aloud what I was thinking. I could only smile for an instant, as the statement made me remember exactly where my ass should be firmly planted.

"If we come under fire, whatever you do, don't jump out of the truck," instructed a young Marine. "There's gonna be so much hot lead coming out of this thing. Outside the truck is the last place you'd want to be," he warned.

The evening ended without violence, but my willingness to put myself in the thick of things gained me entrée into the Los Angeles television market. I went on to become one of the most recognized freelance television journalists in the Southland.

As fate would have it, I was spending the night at my girlfriend's house on Lookout Mountain near Hollywood when the ground began to shake violently. I sprung out of bed, quickly dressed, jumped in my vehicle, rushed down the mountain, and sped down Sunset Boulevard to KTLA fast enough to be one of the first broadcasters on the air after the Landers Quake. From the anchor desk, I informed the city as best I could of the unprecedented strength of the 7.2 mega quake. I reported quake damage alone until the full resources of the station could mobilize.

The *Los Angeles Times'* media section reported Hal Fishman's command of the airwaves on that fateful day. But as I rushed to get off the set and out of the way when the master arrived, Fishman asked me to remain so I could bring him up to speed live on the air.

My ability to keep KTLA ahead of the competition was rewarded with a live truck and two-man crew. I was dispatched to the seismology lab at Cal Tech, where I arrived in time to watch the Richter scale record the magnitude 6.5 Big Bear Quake. It was part two of the now-infamous twin quakes that jolted the Southland on that fateful day. I roamed the back halls of the seismology lab with a science reporter from the *Los Angeles Times*, gathering information well away from the hordes of reporters who waited patiently for updates in the media room. The lab's director spotted us and tore into me like I was a prowler. "What are you doing back here?" he asked in an angry voice. He never addressed the *Times* reporter, but he seemed to be transfixed with me. The way he singled me out, along with his angry unprofessional tone, struck me as racist. I knew he was overwhelmed, but when he asked where I worked, I snapped, brushing him back

"I'm Paul Jackson with KTLA news."

The *Times* reporter, who happened to be white, was never questioned. Before we were interrupted, he informed me of a mathematical formula scientists used that would indicate a potential earthquake swarm, and said they would have to issue what he called an earthquake alert. It was a complex formula dealing with the strength of the quake and its proximity to the San Andreas Fault. The science was sound, and the numbers added up, and before we were asked to return to the media room, I was able to digest most of the formula, which was posted in a lab in the basement. I decided I would use it on the air.

By then, Hal Fishman had the director of the State Emergency Management Agency live on set with him. When they went live to me at Cal Tech, I informed Hal scientists were about to issue an "earthquake alert." The EMA director balked and immediately said that was not true.

"With all due respect, Hal," I replied, "because of the magnitude of the quake and its proximity to the San Andres Fault, scientists have no choice but to issue the alert." At that moment, an entourage of scientists walked in and filled the podium near where I was standing.

Fishman noticed and ended the discussion. We opened the mic to hear Lucy Jones and her colleagues announce, "Southern California has entered an earthquake sequence."

It was one of the most memorable days of my career.

Working at KTLA was a dream come true. As a child, when our family drove to Hollywood, I would search the sky for the station's tower, which displayed its bright neon call letters. In my young mind, it symbolized the gateway to Hollywood. When we drove by KTLA, I wondered what stood behind the magnificent white wall that surrounded two city blocks.

I could hardly believe I was not only behind the great wall, but also working there alongside the very man who filled me with so much pride in my childhood. Larry McCormick, who had long since left KGFJ radio, was a weekend fixture at KTLA TV 5 News.

Back then (it may still be the case today), two sayings resonated with African-American broadcasters. The first was, "Last hired, and first fired." The second was not so much a saying but a reality: weekend shifts were relegated to minorities.

And so on the weekends, I bonded with an African-American freelance photographer by the name of Eric Shinn. Eric and I were both new to the station. We did anything and everything asked of us without so much as a second thought. We were so grateful to work that it took us months to realize we were not being treated like the rest of the staff. We did triple the work, rarely got a lunch break, and were not paid appropriately for our labors.

The two of us knew no fear and quickly became a take-no-prisoners, two-man wrecking crew of weekend news. Correction; on one occasion, we did take a prisoner. With cameras rolling, we orchestrated a fugitive surrender and safely delivered an alleged murder suspect (a teenager who shot his family's landlord in a fit of rage) to LAPD officers awaiting us at the television station.

Eric and I covered breaking news with no regard for our personal safety. No one ever bothered to tell us that there was a clause in the union contract that allowed its members to be awarded hazard pay in certain potentially life-threatening situations. We once rolled up to a flaming railroad tanker. Eric immediately grabbed his camera and moved in closer. I took off to find someone to interview.

When Eric returned, the first thing out of his mouth was, "Man, that was hot! Feel my tripod." I believe I saw smoke floating off the hot metal. In any event, it was too hot to touch. By then, the authorities had arrived and informed us there was a chance the tanker could go at any moment. We were ordered to evacuate to a spot more than a mile away. I think that story would call for hazard pay.

It wasn't always a bed of roses at KTLA. On the advice of a fellow freelance photographer, I grabbed a sixty-minute beta tape from engineering to place my air-checks on. Apparently, freelancers didn't get tapes, so I was asked to return it to the shelf.

The station, meanwhile, had been experiencing an epidemic of petty thefts. Eric told me I'd better have a talk with one of the engineers, who'd accused me of being the thief. I did so immediately. Apparently, someone had walked off with a personal camera that he'd brought to work.

"Well, the janitors weren't here," he said, matter-of-factly. The janitorial staff was entirely Hispanic. "So I figured it had to be you," he concluded.

I gave him a blank stare, unable to speak.

"Well, you're here and you're mad," he added. "So I guess it wasn't you."

Without Eric Shinn looking out for me, I might've never worked another day at KTLA because a white employee was under the impression that only blacks or Hispanics were thieves.

Eric Shinn taught me we (and by we, I mean African-American men) are stronger as a people when we work together as one. We would do anything for one another, and it showed in our work.

Unfortunately, our heroic efforts were not rewarded with staff positions, so I began to freelance for other stations, covering breaking news for KCOP, KTTV, and KCBS. When not on television, I was in high demand as a radio news reporter for KFWB and KNX.

I was the first reporter on the air during the 1994 Northridge earthquake. Reporting from a badly damaged broadcast center at KCBS-TV, I informed the nation that "Southern California has experienced a significant seismic event." I became such a fixture on L.A. Television that I even played myself on the big screen in the motion picture *Jimmy Hollywood*, which starred Joe Pesci and Christian Slater. Though my exceptional work was recognized with an Emmy and the prestigious RTNDA Golden Mic, I was still relegated to freelance status. I eventually left my hometown for a prominent NBC affiliate in northern California after I was offered a staff position with a long-term contract.

CHAPTER 32

SACRAMENTO

When I arrived at KCRA television in Sacramento, California, I was determined to use every tool I learned in Los Angeles, where being first was everything. Eric Shinn and I learned to work fast and take no prisoners. "Get it done or get replaced," was the mantra we were forced to live by.

This way of life didn't go over too well in Sacramento. In fact, I immediately earned the reputation of being an impatient hothead, who could be a bit of a dick. Things were a little more laid-back in the state capital; this top-twenty television market worked more like a small town operation.

What separated me from the crowd in Los Angeles was recognizing early on that it was a market of pack journalists. Most reporters only felt they were doing an adequate job if their stories mirrored those of other stations. Interviews had to be identical, with no divergence from the storyline.

I, however, never accepted that criteria. To me, different was better, and I always strived to produce something different, a story the pack would usually overlook in their race to be the same.

I learned early on never to take sound bites from a news conference podium, unless you are under a tight deadline. In Los Angeles, a tight deadline was to step away from the press conference as it took place and report the story live as it unfolded. This usually happened during the noon news blocks, as producers were hungry for new material.

When a deadline was not looming, I had my photographer record the entire press conference, only to use as background. The pack would decide on a great sound bite from the podium, and you'd hear it on every station in the market. I, meanwhile, pursued my own interviews with the principals after the press conference, by discreetly whisking them away to some remote corner, away from the hordes of media. There, I could have them personally describe the messages they wanted to get across in a conversational and relaxed manner.

I first employed my L.A. tactics at a political rally in Sacramento Valley. My photographer was dumbfounded that he'd recorded an entire press conference, from which I did not intend to use a single word. The very thought offended him.

Following the rally, the candidate was lost in a crowd of humanity. With my obvious height advantage, I could locate him wherever he went in the crowd. Sadly, my photographer, a short, overweight man who stood no more than 5'3", struggled just to carry his camera through the crowd as the politician worked the room. "Man," I thought, "this is like leading a small child by the hand through a crowded amusement park."

My photographer became increasingly frustrated as we chased our intended interview. I had no idea his physical condition would not allow him to continue, as he huffed and puffed through the crowd, finally so out of breath he could not continue another step. He simply gave up as I stood next to the politician as he climbed into his waiting limo.

This was the first indication that perhaps I'd made the wrong decision in coming to Sacramento. It didn't take long to confirm my suspicions. Soon after, I was assigned to cover an inconsequential story, which I don't even recall. What stands out in my mind is, as happens in most newsrooms after the morning meeting, we were running late to a press conference. The photographer I was paired with was hopelessly lost (this was before GPS was commonplace) and pulled over to check the map. Once he realized he was going in the wrong direction, he pulled into a convenience store parking lot to turn around. What happened next leaves me perplexed to this day. Once he turned around, he pulled into a parking space and stopped. Stunned, I inquired, "What are you doing? We are late!"

He looked at me and, in a low-key voice, replied, "I can't make a U-turn in their parking lot without buying something. It's wrong."

Before I could form the words for a reply, he got out of the news cruiser, entered the store, and emerged two minutes later with a pack of gum, offering me a piece before we continued on our way. "Simply unbelievable," I thought.

My final confirmation that I'd arrived on a foreign news planet came shortly after when I was assigned to cover the *San Francisco Chronicle*'s newspaper strike. The paper had gone for days without publishing an issue. But on this morning, an issue written by newspaper management was destined for newsstands.

We made quick time to the Bay area and arrived at the Chronicle building just in time to watch a mob of picketers swarm the gates where a line of delivery trucks were about to exit. As the gates opened and the first truck started easing forward, a riot ensued. Strikers began to pelt the truck wildly with whatever was available to them—sticks, fists, rocks, and bottles. I couldn't believe our good fortune. We'd arrived in time to record this barbarically visual event. Excited, I looked to my photographer, expecting him to pull over, grab his camera, and bail. But to my utter and complete amazement, he continued past the ruckus.

"What are you doing?" I asked, in the midst of a full-blown riot.

He simply said, "I'm looking for a legal parking space."

"Unbelievable! Pop the curb (what we said in L.A. when we parked on the sidewalks) and take the ticket."

I might as well have been speaking Greek. He even refused to let me take the wheel. This blond-haired, blue-eyed do-gooder from Iowa drove past a riot searching for a legal metered parking space. When he finally found one a block away, the trucks had exited, and the riot was over almost as suddenly as it had begun.

In my opinion, one of us didn't get the news business. It was the opinion of that photographer and most of the others on staff that that person was *me*.

There was only one reporter more despised than me. He was a young man in his early twenties who looked much older. He had a full head of hair that was prematurely gray and a face that deceptively appeared as if it had seen a half century of life, not mere decades.

Initially considering him a peer, I jokingly confided with him, "I guess you're the only guy the photogs despise more than me."

I honestly thought we would have a chuckle together. I could not have been more wrong. I suppose I was secretly hoping we would become compadres. To my surprise, this revelation nearly brought the young man to tears. Stunned, he turned to ask the photog I was headed out with whether the statement was true. The photog quietly shook his head in the affirmative.

I learned later that the man I thought a peer was not at all close to my age, but had just turned twenty-four. My respect quickly waned when I realized he was a pretender, and one hell of an impersonator. His only saving grace was that he emulated—in inflection, mannerism, and style one of America's greatest news anchors. This kid had Tom Brokaw down to a science. Though I thought it disingenuous, believing everyone should have a voice of his or her own, young David Gregory chose a most impressive journalist to emulate.

KCRA was one of the most highly respected NBC affiliates in the United States. NBC News Channel, which is based in Charlotte, North Carolina, decided to use the station's resources for breaking news. They called it a regional strike force, and I was to be their primary reporter. Unfortunately, every time they requested my presence, KCRA informed them I was too valuable to daily operations to release. I'd just arrived at KCRA, and management was not in the mood to lose me to the network. When the NBC news channel requested that I cover the O.J. Simpson trial in Los Angeles, their request was again denied. Young David Gregory went in my stead, and the rest, as they say, is history. From that moment on, he was on a network trajectory, and I was relegated to local news in Sacramento. NBC News hired David Gregory after the trial. He was elevated to White House correspondent, and later he hosted *Meet the Press*.

CHAPTER 33

THE MOST DIFFICULT
CHAPTER OF MY LIFE

I n her book *Bird by Bird*, Anne Lamott observes:

We write to expose the unexposed. If there is one door in
the castle you have been told not to go through you must.
Otherwise, you'll just be rearranging furniture in rooms
you've already been in. Most human beings are dedicated
to keeping that one door shut. But the writer's job is to
see what's behind it to see it, to see the bleak
unspeakable stuff, and turn the unspeakable in the words,
not just any words but if we can, in rhythm and blues.

I will now share with you the story I have kept locked away,
hidden in the place where disgrace resides.

While at KCRA-TV, I was asked to voiceover a video that
was to be shown at the Urban League's annual dinner. The
presentation received a huge ovation from the audience and
was apparently the hit of the evening.

Despite all the dignitaries present, the event photographer
seemed to be taking an extraordinary interest in my family
and me. She followed me around the event and photographed
me as if I were the head of the Urban League. Then I noticed
she was using the same brand camera as I'd treated myself to
a few days earlier. Unfortunately, I really had no idea how to
use the camera since most of its advanced functions left me

perplexed. Gazing at her equipment, which was far more complex than mine was, I shared with her that I had a camera just like hers, and though it could perform a multitude of functions, I was barely able to take a photograph. It was frustrating me, and I wondered whether I'd wasted my money so I was considering returning the camera.

She assured me that it would be fairly easy to learn, and she offered to bring me up to speed with a free lesson on how to use it. I readily agreed, and we exchanged phone numbers.

After the event, my wife, Amy, made it a point to speak with me about the photographer, telling me there was something not quite right with her. Amy had noticed that she was taking far too great an interest in our family and me, and she warned me away from the lessons. Even then, there was a feeling welling up inside me—the knowing—that she was probably correct. But the fact that my camera was advertised as a simple point-and-shoot, yet its technology was still too advanced, frustrated me to no end, so I thought there must be an easier way to use it.

Against my better judgment, I contacted the photographer to take her up on her lesson. She assured me the camera was fairly easy to operate, and I should have no problem. We made small chat about life, and I ended the conversation by telling her I'd call her back when I could come up with a good time we could meet.

When I called her a few days later, she asked me to come to her apartment, which I did. The moment I entered, I knew something was amiss. The living room section of the apartment was empty. There was no couch or chairs, just the table. And on top of the table were several nude photos of her. I've done all in my power to scratch any and all images of this woman from my mind. I recall her as being 5'7", very attractive, yet extremely skinny. She had blonde hair, but I couldn't begin to tell you what her face looked like or the color of her eyes. As you have learned about me in this book, I have an instinct, "a knowing," for avoiding danger. The voice in my head was speaking to me loud and clear: leave this place now; this is wrong. I chose not to listen.

I couldn't help but comment on the only conversation pieces in the room. I found the nude photos arousing and concluded anyone who would present this image of herself probably had just one thing in mind, and now it was on my mind. I now assumed her special interest in me was purely physical and, against my better judgment, I tested the theory. My embrace led us to the only furniture in her home, which was a bed in her bedroom. I felt tremendous trepidation the moment I entered; unfortunately, my hormones and insatiable sex drive were coming to the forefront, leaving reason behind. As we lay in bed together, I knew it was wrong. That is when events turned psychotic.

When engaged in a petting session, I got a stronger "knowing" that I was in the wrong place. Her behavior seemed almost bipolar, as if I were in the room with two different people. One moment she would draw me close for my affections, but when I reciprocated, she would query, "What are you doing?"

"Destroying my marriage and my life," I thought to myself. I immediately decided it was time to leave. As bizarre as things had seemed to me until that point, they were about to get even more crazy. A look of sheer panic filled her face. She pushed me hard onto the bed and began to rub my penis furiously through my pants. Then she began to cry out, "Is this what you want? Is *this* what you want?"

I'm embarrassed to say I was lost in the erotic insanity of the moment and began to orgasm.

This time when she asked, "What are you doing?" I regained my senses and finally realized I was in the presence of a true lunatic. I cleaned myself with a washcloth she had given me and excused myself. She walked me out of her apartment and into the parking lot. I gave her an embrace and we said our goodbyes with my camera on my shoulder; it'd never left its case.

By now, my inner voice was screaming at me. "You ignored the sacred warning. Now you must live with the consequences." My inner voice has never been wrong.

Soon after, the photographer began to call me at work. Her conversations were hard to follow, and I rushed her off the line by telling her I would call her later. When I had a moment of privacy, I contacted her. She asked me why I did that. I asked, "What?" And so began a game of verbal cat and mouse.

She indicated that I had somehow taken advantage of her. I panicked, thinking this was the *knowing* I had been warned of, and I would lose my wife and family as a result. I tried to calm her and appease her in any way that would keep her away from me. During the course of the conversation, I heard voices in the background and instantly knew what was happening. The police were on the line and she was being coached in how to get me to say I had assaulted her. When I realized this, I piped in to remind her that she'd masturbated me through my pants. She began to cry and say it wasn't true. Her response mortified me. I was sure her intent was to ruin my marriage for whatever sinister reason she possessed.

When I lived in Tulsa, I had dated a federal judge. I thought back to the evening she had cautioned me to be wary of this exact scenario. "Sinister people will go out of their way to discredit a black man," she warned, "especially a television personality. Don't mess with white women."

The guilt of my indiscretion superseded all judgment. In my mind, I was a guilty man. Not of sexual assault, but I was guilty of being a disloyal husband. I decided I must do all in my power to shield my family, and the best way to do it was to try to appease a psychotic.

Later that evening, I got a call from the public information officer of the Sacramento Sheriff's Department. He wanted me to come in to talk. He simply stated, "I think you know what it's about."

I waited alone in the lobby of the Sacramento Sheriff's Department for almost an hour before I was escorted to an interrogation room. There, two detectives interviewed me for the better part of an hour. They played good cop, bad cop in hopes of catching me in a lie, but my story never wavered because it was the truth.

In an attempt to show me they'd done a thorough job on my background check, one of the officers informed me that I was liked by law enforcement in Los Angeles, but fired from KTLA for releasing sensitive information about a bank robbery. I knew exactly what they were talking about, but I'd not been fired from KTLA. I explained, "You can't fire a freelancer." The L.A.P.D. had given me sensitive information about the contents of a pack of money taken in a robbery. It had been rigged with an explosive dye pack. I passed that information on to my producer, expressly telling him the information was not for broadcast, at the request of law enforcement. His response was, "Fuck the police." It was now abundantly clear that when police came down on KTLA for releasing that information, blame was promptly handed down to me. It was the first I'd ever known of law enforcement's dissatisfaction with one of my news reports.

My interrogation was one-sided. The sad part is I considered myself guilty. Not guilty of a crime, but guilty of ignoring my inner voice, the knowing, that has been guiding me throughout life. I was also guilty of displaying horrible judgment. Guilty of cheating on my wife. And guilty of being a bad father. It is safe to say I did not defend myself to my fullest abilities. In fact, in regards to the telephone call, the "good cop" expressed my feelings for me saying, "So when you called, you would have said yes to anything in an attempt to keep her away from your wife." His observation was right on target. It is impossible to be indignant while at the same time feeling embarrassed because you have done something wrong, in this case breaking a sacred trust.

After they'd heard enough, I was allowed to leave. They told me their findings would be passed on to the District Attorney's Office to decide whether charges should be filed.

Sgt. McGinnis, the public information officer, walked me out. McGinnis and I were partners in a delicate dance between law enforcement and the news media.

I had arrived in Sacramento with the seal of approval from Los Angeles County Sherriff Sherman Block. I won his vote of confidence when I pulled him aside after a press conference to relay complaints from my neighbors in Carson about deputies camping out at the intersection of Turmont and Central Avenues, issuing hundreds of traffic citations each week to residents, most or all of whom were African Americans. The day after I informed Sherriff Block, deputies stopped issuing traffic citations there.

Since I considered Sgt. McGinnis a friend, I asked him what he thought. His reply was sharp and to the point. "I think you got set up by a crazy psycho bitch," he answered. And as was his tradition of sharing sensitive information with me, he informed me that the Sacramento Sheriff's Department knew her. This was her modus operandi. "She's done this three other times, all to police officers," he said. "Regardless of her history, the department has an obligation to investigate."

The guilt of what I'd done overwhelmed me. The trauma of being interviewed by the police and accused of what they termed a misdemeanor sexual assault could all but kill my career as a journalist. I confessed my transgression to my wife, and I told her of my interview with the sheriff. She apparently had a knowing, too. She said, "I told you to stay away from that woman; something was wrong with her. She saw a perfect family and wanted to destroy it."

For whatever reason, Amy knew why a woman with unsavory designs somehow lured me in. She would not divorce me and remained by my side.

I called my friend Leo Terrell, a prominent civil rights attorney in Los Angeles. We'd gone to high school together. His first advice was not to speak to the police about anything, under *any circumstances*. When I informed him it was a little late for that, he told me it was *their* job to find me guilty. "They are not your friends," he said, adding I should end all conversation with them. He would reach out to the District Attorney's Office in the interim.

I sought psychological counseling for the stress of being interrogated by law enforcement and for the future possibility of charges and an arrest. During the counseling session, my wife brought up the woman I'd dated before I met her.

She was an aspiring Hollywood actress. A vivacious redhead, with stunning good looks. In fact, I was drawn to her physically long before we began to experience each other mentally. We had a relationship that was built solely on sex. She was completely uninhibited, and displayed all the characteristics of a nymphomaniac. As far as I was concerned, she was the perfect woman. After just a couple of months of this whirlwind romance, I was addicted to her love and we moved in together, sharing an apartment on the water in Marina Del Rey. Shortly after, she began to reveal strange life secrets, and our relationship began to unravel. I learned she was a former Rockette and a "kept woman." An elderly man who lived in New York was financing her apartment. Despite the fact that he was married, they had a long running relationship that lasted many years. This didn't sit well with me, and I asked her to stop taking his money.

"Why? I only have to give him a blow job once or twice a year," she responded matter-of-factly. I was sick and knew our relationship was over. I later found out that as stunning as she was, she was fifteen years older than I was, and no longer capable of having children. Entering this relationship, I was very clear that I wanted to have a family one day. I found the stories she told me of her personal life sadly repulsive. She explained she'd been raped dozens of times. Her first lover was her dance instructor, who had taken her virginity at the age of thirteen. I found an inexpensive apartment nearby and began the process of moving out. She was at home one afternoon when I was picking up the last of my things, so I decided to try for a final roll in the hay. She was resistant, but I knew all the right buttons to push, so we ended our relationship on a highly kinky note, having sex in a walk-in closet where the last of my clothes were.

Apparently feeling scorned, she accused me of sexual assault. I never gave her accusation a second thought. Sure, I was aggressive, but how, I wondered could someone claim she was assaulted yet experience multiple orgasms so powerful that neighbors could hear her passion?

It was the last time I saw her, but I understand that she went on to write a one-woman show; much of it had to do with being raped dozens of times.

I told Amy about my former roommate's accusation when we began dating. But I failed to mention the part about multiple orgasms. Amy relayed the story to my therapist. He had no words. After listening carefully, his advice was to go to my employers immediately and tell them what was going on. He added that they probably already knew.

When I spoke to my news director, Bill Bauman, he slammed the door to his office and called the general manager. "He's here; come in," he said. "I've been waiting for you. What took you so long?" He said my accuser had called the assistant news director days ago and accused me of sexual assault. The assistant news director convened a meeting of the department heads. Moreover, explained Bauman, he'd been the one to report the incident to the sheriff's department.

Bauman again grabbed his telephone and this time told the GM not to come to his office. I told my side of the story, or at least as much as he wanted to hear, and alerted him to the potential legal charges ahead. He understood the tremendous amount of stress I was under and told me to take the day off to be with my family.

Over the next two weeks, I became a different man. I lost all confidence and second-guessed myself on every story that had to do with law enforcement. Though I did not ask, I felt as if one of the managers had leaked this sensitive information about me, and many members of the news department now considered me a deviant.

The strangest part of the story is, I was simply left there to hang in the unknowing. It seems the District Attorney's Office had no interest in filing charges of any kind because of the woman's history. It was a case of "he said/she said," and obviously, I was the more believable. It seems everyone but me knew she was unbalanced and should be avoided at all cost. I surmised this when the "bad cop" asked me to meet him and informed me there would be no charges brought against me. Then, out of the blue, he turned to ask me, "What really happened?"

Leo was right. Though I'd sat with them, telling the truth, the whole truth, and nothing but the truth, this guy didn't believe me. I gave him a look that required no answer. He quickly relented. "Okay, okay," he said as I turned my back and we went our separate ways.

What I wanted to say was, "She is a liar." I would never do that, and here are the reasons why:

When I was in the fifth grade, a new development went up behind our house called Leadership Homes. It was another situation where African-Americans were "dissuaded" from buying homes, until someone went to court to force the issue. Our new neighbors were all white, and the color line was my street. I made friends with the Nixon family, who were white. They had four boys; I was in the Scouts with two of them. I spent a lot of time playing in their front yard, admiring the beautiful young mother across the street. She was friendly and had two young children. She always said hello to me, and I to her.

One night, I was awakened by screams. "Stop! Please stop! Somebody help me!"

The cries were coming from down the hill. Paula and I convened in my mother's bedroom to hear what was going on. We looked out the window to the homes below, but we could see nothing. The screams became louder and more terrifying. "Somebody help! Oh God, somebody please help me!" she cried.

Paula became unraveled and broke down into tears. "Mommy, please do something," she pleaded.

As my mother called the police, I realized where the cries for help were coming from. It was the home of the young mother I adored so much. She was being gang raped by two neighborhood boys. I saw Mr. Nixon come out of his house and step onto his front lawn as neighbors began to assemble outside. They all stood listening, but no one helped. No one ran to her house to kick down the front door as her desperate cries for help continued.

I could bear the sound no longer. I retrieved my BB gun and my dog. I would rescue her myself if the adults could not.

"Paul! What are you doing?" my mother screamed at the top of her lungs. "You're not going over there."

I don't know how long we endured her cries for help. I do know I will never forget them or the anguish I felt that night. I felt anger and helplessness. How could anyone perform such a barbaric act on such a beautiful woman?

At that moment, I vowed that when I grew up, if I ever heard or witnessed a rape, I would kill the attacker.

Years later, a close relative revealed she'd been raped at gunpoint while on a date in college.

"Who did it?" I asked.

"Paul, no," she replied.

I began to weep. "Who did it?" I asked with tears now rolling down my face. Though I was still young and skinny, she clearly knew what my intention was. I begged her to tell me who her attacker was, but she would not.

I envisioned a plan in which I would wait for him outside his apartment, and then ambush him with a hammer. Once I brought him down, I planned to crush his testicles so he could never hurt anyone again.

I would tell that doubting sheriff's deputy that a relative likely saved me from a jail term or worse by keeping the identity of her rapist to herself. I would tell him that to this day, I can still hear my neighbor pleading for her life as she was brutalized. I can see my relative surrendering at gunpoint.

These are not healthy images to hold in one's mind for a lifetime, which is why I chose to bury these life traumas deep within. Do you want the truth? I despise rapists and believe they should be dealt with in the harshest possible way. This is the truth, the whole truth, and nothing but the truth, so help me God.

That's what I wanted to tell him…. Now you know.

Since my three-year contract was up with the television station, we decided it best to leave this market, and this nightmare, behind. Yet with all the faith and spirituality I possessed, I was never able to forgive myself for this transgression. I mean, how stupid can a man be? I carried this burden to our new home and my next job. It overwhelmed me with paranoia, and when anything went wrong professionally, I instantly assumed it was all based on this singular incident. My self-loathing and lack of confidence eventually destroyed my marriage, and almost ended my career in broadcasting.

I thought time would heal the dark secret. But only maturity brings the realization that time cannot heal the soul. Thankfully, our souls do not record time; they record growth.

CHAPTER 34

OHANA

"Ohana means family. No one is forgotten, or left behind."

— From the movie *Lilo & Stitch*

"Parents are the ultimate role models for children. Every word, movement, and action has an effect. No other person or outside force has a greater influence on a child than the parent."

— Bob Keeshan, who entertained and educated generations of children as television's Captain Kangaroo

My saving grace were my children. Our first, Katelyn Imani, was born in Sacramento. Ours being my wife Amy who miraculously appeared in my life, soon after I learned my girlfriend (the aspiring actress I was shacking up with in a cozy waterside apartment in the marina) was a kept woman.

The first time I met Amy, she came off as a bit too sparky for my taste. I was on assignment with KCOP-TV 13 Los Angeles and had just returned from a long day in Solano County retracing the final days of Cesar Chavez. The legendary civil rights activist had passed away a day earlier of unspecified natural causes after ending a fast in San Luis, Arizona. I was proud of the obituary I wrote, and I left the finished product in Amy's capable hands to write the anchor lead.

The moment I left the building, Amy was told to trim some time off my masterpiece, which, in her defense, was excessively long by news standards. Passionate about my piece, I wrongly thought that by the simple virtue of Chavez being the father of the United Farm Workers, his story surely would deem extra care and airtime. It did not.

And so it was a contentious beginning when my producer (Amy) asked me, "Do you want to go out on a date."

"Ah, sure! Yes!"

We met at Cha-Cha-Cha, a beautiful Caribbean restaurant, off hip and trendy Melrose in Los Angeles.

I saw Amy in a different light that night. I was mesmerized by her energy and looks. I quivered when I learned she was just twenty-six-years old. As it happened, it was my birthday, and I was celebrating thirty-eight. I did not intend to tell Amy about my birthday, but as it turned out, this inquisitive producer already knew, and when our server brought the bill, she did not intend to let me pay. "Happy Birthday," she said.

We spent the rest of the evening crisscrossing popular L.A. nightclubs...and making out. Amy later confided she was skeptical and took everything I said with a grain of salt, because she was well aware I was still living with my girlfriend in the marina.

By the end of the week, I'd found a tiny apartment off Pacific Avenue, just a stone's throw from Ocean Front Walk.

The selling points were the price of rent, parking, an enclosed garage, and oh yes, the beach as your backyard. Thankfully, the owner was anxious to rent, and since he had seen me on TV, he discarded his other applications and let me in right away.

I was living a dream there on the beach with the rich and famous. One of my neighbors was actor Dudley Moore. The star of the movies *10* and *Arthur*, the media referred to Moore as the sex thimble, in reference to his short stature and reputation as a lady's man. He was having a tumultuous relationship with a single mother who lived up the street. After a night of heavy drinking, the couple got into a scrap. Moore was arrested and spent the night in jail. Since I knew where he lived, KTLA assigned me to cover the story. It was strange to ring my neighbor's doorbell as a reporter. Moore spoke to me over an intercom, and as you might expect, had no comment.

Amy and I had an enchanted courtship at my little beach pad. I got to know her and her dog, a handsome Rhodesian ridgeback/Carolina hound rescue whose name happened to be Jaxon. *Cue eerie music in the background.*

It was like that from the beginning between us. I found the fact that she stated aloud my exact thoughts, word for word, disconcerting... frightening even. When we weren't reading each other's thoughts, she was moving household items to the exact spot where I was about to move them. We thought and verbalized seemingly random thoughts together all the time. In fact, our constant mental synchronization made it feels sometimes as if we were of one mind.

Six months after meeting her, I found myself kneeling on one knee, my back to the ocean with a diamond ring in my hand. I'd never experienced this kind of mental connection.

But I relished the feeling of being drawn to Amy's mind. It was not until after we were married I would make the mind-body connection. After the first days of our honeymoon, I wondered where the brainy Ivy League journalism graduate I married went. Though she looks African American, Amy is biracial, and after just two days on Maui, her skin took on a golden hue I had no idea existed. The surf and sun washed her hair, and the curves of her bikini were exquisite. Gazing upon her overwhelmed my senses. I wondered, "How could I have married one of the most attractive women on the planet and not have noticed until now?"

I could not take my eyes off my new bride. And when I did for just one moment.... Boy, did she let me have it. I was walking past a small television set that one of the fulltime residents of the condo we'd rented had placed outside. One look, and I was locked in and glued to breaking news. It was O.J. Simpson in the infamous low-speed chase. Moreover, it was my assigned shift (which I'd forfeited for my honeymoon) at KTTV Los Angeles.

"Oh no, you are not watching news on our honeymoon," Amy said loudly, pulling me away from the set, and so it was that O.J. Simpson and his big story alluded me...from the beginning.

Now, our first, Katelyn Imani, was born in Sacramento.

Before I became a father, television news was my life. As a freelance journalist in Los Angeles, I regularly worked twelve-hour days with no complaint. My friend Eric Shinn and I had a motto, "Take the money." We lived with our pagers on our belts and never turned down an assignment or opportunity to put in some overtime.

On January 17, 1994, not more than an hour after the Northridge earthquake, after dodging falling debris from crumbling light fixtures in the KCBS-TV Newsroom, I hijacked a live truck.

Let me take a breath and back up. I had an a.m. call time for a per diem shift at KCBS-TV. When we finished our shift in the early afternoon, the newsroom scanners were buzzing on all frequencies with news of a car chase. I always volunteered for breaking news. The chase began in Sacramento and I, yes, *I* was driving the live truck, so my photog (who happened to be a woman) could gear up.

She was on her way out the door when the assignment desk changed her plans. We intercepted the pursuit and joined the tail end of what was a long precession of flashing red lights on surface streets in downtown L.A. The driver suddenly pulled to the side and bailed. We pulled up close behind and jumped out of our live truck. *Bang, bang!* I took cover behind the door after I heard gunfire and saw a young white male blasting his way through glass doors and into a federal building, where he took a security guard hostage.

When I looked to my right, I saw my photographer standing fearlessly in the open. She got it all on tape. The suspect surrendered, after the 11 p.m. newscast.

"Hey, guys," a female voice said over the two-way as we were packing up to return to the station. "Great stuff. CBS asked if you could package it for the morning news."

Who turns down the network?

We were laying in the last edit to this story at 4:30 a.m. when the studio began to shake violently. I looked at my editor as a crescendoing rumble broke the silence. The soundproof glass in our edit bay began to bow to the shattering point when we finally stood and headed for the door. Interior lights in the studio were arcing, producing a surreal scene as the sparks flew. Dust particles falling from the rattling fixtures filled the air, producing an eerie psychedelic effect. Making our way to the door, I had to use the illuminated exit sign as a marker as studio cameras tipped and fell around us. When we emerged outside, I was amazed to find the entire news staff had left the building.

Being the only reporter present, I knew I must seize the moment.

"Okay, let's get back inside and get on the air," I said bravely. I was still (pardon the pun) quaking in my boots as I observed dozens of bricks had been dislodged from the building exactly where we were standing. I instantly realized why safety experts warn that you should resist the urge to run outside during an earthquake.

Once back inside, the damage was shocking; the studio was toast. The AM producer took charge and asked me to broadcast from an old sound booth, no larger than 8"x10". It was a lost relic of the '70s, hidden in a tiny dark corner of the station. I never knew it existed. One emergency light on the ceiling provided illumination so I was not completely in the dark, and the producer joined me in my ear. I did my best to compose myself, though I felt as if I were inside a tomb.

"Southern California has experienced a significant seismic event," were the first words I could utter. I'd theorized if the station's location were near the epicenter, then it was possible not everyone in our viewing area felt the event. I was wrong! It turned out to be 6.7 on the Richter scale.

I explained our studio had been damaged, then began improvising on CalTrans safety protocols. I had most of the agencies' disaster and emergency response procedures memorized, and I did my best to sound reassuring, though I was horrified. I was sure a strong aftershock would bury me there.

Finally, someone thought of using the mounted traffic camera, which was located upstairs in a KNX radio studio. Radio traffic reporter Jill Angel took over the station's coverage and I hustled outside.

"You're with me," I told my photographer from the previous day. She simply assumed the assignment desk paired us together. In actuality, I'd hijacked her and the live truck during the confusion.

When we pulled out of the studio lot, I saw looters tearing into a Hollywood grocery store. Another point on the Richter scale, I thought, and we'd be looking at a complete breakdown of society. We drove by the looters, without a second thought, but their image stuck in my mind. At that moment, I decided to become a gun owner, believing it would be better to have a gun than to need it and not to have it.

We followed plumes of smoke from erupting natural gas lines to Studio City. We drove up into the hills for a better view, but we were stopped by a line of emergency vehicles on a narrow street. When we got out and walked toward the ruckus, I saw a man sitting on the curb with a blanket around him.

"Are you okay?" I asked.

He went on to explain that he had woken up to his house tumbling down the hillside. The violent shaking tore his home from its foundation. He described what happened in vivid detail, saying he was literally swimming up through the debris as his home disintegrated around him. He was obviously in shock, but I think talking with us helped.

After I interviewed him, I pointed him out to authorities to make sure he got medical attention. Someone once told me they saw me on the History Channel sitting next to a man on a curb wrapped in a blanket. Now you know the rest of the story.

Taking a breath, I remembered Amy.... My God, AMY! I rushed to the cell phone in the live truck.

"Your neon palm tree broke," she said in a calm voice. She was not in the least bit worried because I had not checked in. She knew where I had to be, on this story. Amy was a journalist. She weathered the quake alone with no fear. When I knew she was safe, I continued my forty-eight-hour on-air marathon.

Never in my life did I ever dream anything would be more important than journalism, until I witnessed the birth of my daughter. The moment I laid eyes on her, everything else became secondary.

Upon her birth, I took advantage of the family leave act (which, coincidentally, was co-authored by my Denver poolside friend, Congresswoman Pat Schroeder) and left my job for an entire month so I could bond with my newborn daughter.

Before my daughter entered this world, I immersed myself in parenting courses and was envious to learn newborns imprinted on their mothers during their first days, especially if they were breast-fed as my daughters were. In my limited experience, fathers were hardly seen and I was determined to change that and become an equal partner in every aspect of early child rearing. I can remember Katelyn's first night home like it was yesterday. I took her out of the bassinette at our bedside and placed her on my bare chest so she could see my face, feel my warmth and touch, and most of all, hear the sound of my heartbeat. She was still learning to breathe, and I was so worried, occasionally nudging her in her sleep to make her take a breath.

I encourage all fathers to link with newborns in this way. The two of us now share a bond that I truly believe will never be broken.

When I returned to reporting, I discovered I had changed. I was less willing to risk life or limb. Before Katelyn, homicides rarely fazed me, but now murders, particularly those involving children, really began to take a psychological toll. I began to see the victims I interviewed as people, and I became less willing to exploit their pain. The adrenaline rush I'd long associated with covering breaking news no longer made me high.

I wasn't losing my edge, but I was changing. There was something about me I just couldn't put my finger on...and then it hit me. I was a parent!

Katelyn was walking by nine months; at one year, she was running. She frightened us when she became a toddler because she would lean forward until almost falling on her face, then run as fast as she could to catch her body. She became a high school All American in track.

Kyra Skye arrived sixteen months later. This was after we'd been informed Amy should've changed her birth control prescription after she stopped breast-feeding. While Katelyn literally and figuratively came out the womb at warp speed, our second happy arrival had a tough start. She was a breech baby. Katelyn's arrival had gone smoothly, so doctors cut Kyra's umbilical cord, which was wrapped around her neck, before she was delivered.

It proved to be a critical mistake since this was a much longer delivery than the first. I followed in horror as nurses took her into the hallway, calling a code blue. Just as the crash team arrived, my little girl took her first breath, and she has been going strong ever since.

We raised our daughters as water babies; they could swim before they could walk. I wanted our California transplants (who were now Philadelphia girls) to see firsthand where I'd grown up. I chose Redondo Beach, a favorite hangout from my high school days.

As my wife and I settled in on the beach, Katelyn (then age six) and her little sister Kyra took off into the water like the little fish we raised them to be. They had no fear of the ocean and no knowledge of the Pacific.

On hot summer days, Kyra would line little boys up and race them across the neighborhood pool. None of them could understand how a girl could possibly beat them, so they raced until they could swim no more.

Somehow, Katelyn had gotten her hands on a boogie board. She hopped on and began to paddle out to sea. I was obliviously setting up my beach chair when I heard my wife calling her name. The seas were rough, with waves breaking at three to five feet due to the remnants of a hurricane that was striking Mexico's Baja Peninsula. When I looked up, Katelyn was in an area of the ocean where I knew she could not touch the bottom. A split second later, a huge swell began to form behind her. After that moment of utter shock and sheer panic, I kicked off my shoes to go in after her. I knew it wouldn't be possible to reach her before the mountainous wave pushed her to the ocean floor. In that moment of madness, something happened that neither my wife nor I expected. As the wave approached, Katelyn skillfully turned her board, caught the wave, and rode it all the way back to shore as if she had done it a million times before.

Perhaps we should have named her Ariel, from *The Little Mermaid*, since this would be only the first of many harrowing adventures she would have in the deep blue sea.

While we were on vacation in Hawaii, Kyra splashed around us like a dolphin at play as we explored the depths of Honolua Bay. I became over-confident with the girls' prowess in the ocean. I allowed Katelyn to swim in the ocean alone (in front of us, of course) while we took a breather. As we relaxed in the warm sand, she swam farther out.

Amy asked, "Are you concerned about Katelyn?"

"No," I replied, as Katelyn continued to push herself out to sea.

Then Amy demanded, "Paul, you'd better go get her!"

As I stumbled around on the beach, trying to put on my heavy diver fins, Katelyn was going farther out, and I grew extremely concerned. Caught in a time warp, believing I was still a young and spry freshman at the University of Hawaii, I swam toward her at a brisk pace. And then—don't you know it?—I caught a leg cramp that stopped me dead in the water. When I looked up, I was relieved to see that a diver had Katelyn safely in tow. She was hugging her boogie board when he handed her over.

"She was kind of far out there," he said.

"Yeah, I know. Thank you *very* much," I replied, the bad parent.

As we returned to shore, I floated on my back with Katelyn tucked at my side. I asked, "Katelyn, why did you go out so far?"

She told me she was trying to leave the harbor so she could body surf (as she'd done in Redondo Beach) the breakers just outside the bay.

Surfers consider Oahu's famous Banzai Pipeline, with its mountainous waves, the original Hawaiian roller-coaster ride. But for land-lovers, Maui's Route 360 is the ticket. Known to the world as The Road to Hana, breathtaking vistas enliven the senses around every one of its 112 turns. When you travel east, spectacular waterfalls capture passengers' side views, while rocky cliffs overhanging the deep blue Pacific occupy the driver's view. Around almost every bend, danger lurks as land sharks sometimes fishtail out of their lanes for a close encounter of the worst kind with oncoming traffic.

Weary of tourists and their propensity for stopping on blind curves to snap a few photos, I decided we should escape by (pardon the cliché) taking the road less traveled—an unmarked trail somewhere past Mile Post Three—which led to what promised to be a secluded beach below. Less than fifty yards off The Hana Highway, we were enveloped by lush jungle vegetation. The road narrowed to a tight trail that looked as if it doubled as a riverbed when clouds in the rainforest above let go. The gravelly descent prompted me to disengage the rented Jeep Grand Cherokee's autotrack system for the psychological security of fulltime four-wheel drive. As we emerged from a tunnel of thick vines and native foliage, I was a bit frazzled to see a sheer cliff and the ocean several hundred feet below. My family freaked out at the site. Though this was far from my first time adventuring off road (I have taken several off road driving lessons in the mountains of Southern California), I began to feel that this impromptu excursion wasn't such a bright idea and began to look ahead for a safe spot to turn around. After creeping forward for what felt like a mile, but was actually about 100 yards, I spotted a clearing wide enough to turn around and abort our excellent adventure. The only obstacles in our path were two boulders, one too wide to drive around, the other a little too tall to straddle. I would have to climb over them.

I turned to my wife and told her that she would have to get out and spot me. Her blank expression told the rest of the story; she had no idea what I was talking about. I explained that she needed to make sure my tires were where they needed to be, since I had no desire to get stuck in an area where I was uninsured and contractually forbidden to enter. Yes, not only was this excellent adventure ill advised, it was also illegal. Most standard rental agreements state that you may not take a rental vehicle onto a road that is unpaved.

Though hopping these volcanic rocks would be little to ask of our trail-rated rental, if my spotter and I were not precise, I could easily crease the rig on the rocks or, worse yet, damage the undercarriage.

Caught up in the excitement of being out of bounds and fantasizing about the wonders of the beach below, I knew exactly what I had to do. I took a deep breath, grasped the floor-mounted shifter, slammed our Jeep into low range, slowly shifted into reverse, and then crawled back out to the highway.

We made it to Hana, where Katelyn and Kyra got to see the end of a Hana junior lifeguard practice. By then, they looked like sun-kissed locals. When a lifeguard saw us, he asked whether they wanted to ride in the rescue sled. They agreed, and he took them on a wild Jet Ski ride over the bay. It was a bit more than they bargained for, but the reward was at the end of the ride when they learned they'd become official junior lifeguards.

Though somewhat dangerous, our short time off the beaten path left us longing for more alone time.

So after a pleasant lunch and an afternoon swim in Hana Bay, we continued our trek, circling the entire island, sections of which were unpaved. In some stretches, there was not a soul around us for miles. This section of Route 360, conveniently omitted from our map, is one of the most beautiful drives in the world. In an instant, you drop out of a tropical mountain rainforest into cattle country. A few miles later, the scenery changes back to ocean views so magnificent they boggle the mind.

As we continued the search for less aggressive trails to the sea, we made a surprising discovery; it seemed "wilds" were off limits. Jeep trails, which were easy to find, were either chained off or posted closed. They were *kapu*—the Hawaiian word for keep out—not only to tourists, but to local motion as well.

Eventually, we discovered what appeared to be a user-friendly road at the end of Kings Trail, on the south side of the island, near Nukuele Point. There we found something a bit more ominous than chains or the posted closure signs. We saw two words that strike fear in the heart of even the most experienced off-road trekkers: "Road impassable," read the sign.

"Yeah," I thought. "Maybe for a Mini Cooper." Still, the gargantuan volcanic rocks that lined the side of this road made me err on the side of caution. I flagged down a local who was motoring past the warning signs in a Jeep Cherokee.

"Is the road tough up ahead?" I asked.

"Nah, not a problem," he said in a thick Pidgin English accent. "I come here to fish almost every day and never get stuck. I don't even have four-wheel drive," he added with a broad smile.

"Many roads on the island are being closed to SUVs," said another Hawaiian native we met. He rolled in, in a 1987 Jeep Cherokee Laredo with a two-inch lift. His bed was filled with colorful fish, some of which were still alive. "A lot of private construction companies are buying the land and closing the roads for private developments," he complained. "You won't get stuck here. They put up these signs to keep the tourists out."

I knew exactly what I had to do. I took a deep breath, slammed the Jeep into four-wheel drive, but this time...I went for it. After all, life's a beach!

CHAPTER 35

FAMOUS PEOPLE

I'd wager a pretty penny that somewhere during the course of your life, you've met a celebrity. When we do, that encounter usually becomes a benchmark in our life story. The mere mention of the person's name opens a beaker of vivid memories.

Such remembrance either leaves us diminished, in a state of joy, or somewhere in between—depending, of course, on the depth and breadth of the encounter.

When I was no more than six years old, I met actor John Forsyth at an autograph session at Compton High School. I assume he was at the school to promote his television sitcom, *Bachelor Father*. Forsyth played a single playboy, Bentley Gregg, who assumes the responsibility of raising his niece after her parents die in a car crash.

I loved the show, and I had a crush on Kelly (Noreen Corcoran), his television niece. Compton High seemed like a strange place for a Hollywood superstar to be signing autographs, but there he was. I remember standing by his side at the table where dozens of adoring fans were lined up to get his autograph. All the while, I chatted with him. We had a splendid conversation, and although I don't recall what we talked about, I remember he looked at me closely and listened to every word I said. He answered every question I asked as if I were an adult.

"Do you really kiss those girls on TV?" I asked, giggling.

Forsyth gave a big smile and told me I'd have to come visit him in Hollywood.

During that micro-span of my life, John Forsyth taught me I was somebody. "He's different," I thought. There he was at Compton High School, surrounded by Negroes. And then it came to me: John Forsyth wasn't prejudiced. I held on to that thought and the friendship he offered to a six-year-old boy that night, and tucked it away. I was friends with a Hollywood star who saw me as me. Not as a little black boy from Compton. But just a boy. It was an empowering celebrity encounter I will never forget.

CHAPTER 36

Q

I was enchanted by the grandeur as I stood before the amazing fountain on the Avenue of the Stars, near Century Plaza Hotel. Newly hired at the OCN, my general manager, Ken Tiven, wholeheartedly approved me attending the National Association of Black Journalists' annual convention, which was being held at the Century Plaza.

I'd driven from Santa Ana and felt a bit overwhelmed at the opening reception. To collect my thoughts, I retreated into a courtyard within the hotel to hide out. I was unaware of the two men standing just a few feet away.

When I finally looked up and glimpsed their faces, I realized I'd wandered into what appeared to be a very private powwow between Quincy Jones and the Rev. Jesse Jackson. Embarrassed, awestruck, and startled, I apologized for interrupting and backed away like a servant leaving royalty. Before I had a chance to disappear into the woodwork, Quincy Jones looked up and hit me with a broad smile as if he had known me all my life. He motioned for me to come over and join them. I could barely speak my name when Jones jumped in.

He was like an inquisitive uncle—wanting details of your life, trying to glimpse a sense of who you were, as a person, leaving no opening that would allow you to be awed by his colossal stardom, let alone his influence on black culture.

Rev. Jackson stood close by, observing carefully. I awkwardly explained that I was a television journalist at the fledgling Orange County News Channel. What happened next was, at least in my eyes, purely remarkable, as Rev. Jackson took a nurturing tone, stepped in close, and offered his hand, "Call me if you need anything," he said as he wrote down his personal telephone number. And while I sensed the offer came with the utmost sincerity, I could also tell he was anxious to continue the confab he and Q were so clearly involved in before I stumbled upon them.

It was a close encounter of the best kind.

I had a close celebrity encounter of the worst kind with actor LeVar Burton. If looks could kill, his probably would, I thought, following a brief encounter with him while strolling along the Third Street Promenade on the Santa Monica Mall one warm summer evening. I looked up, and was astounded to see the star of *Roots* standing in front of me. I rushed over, intending to tell him how much I enjoyed his work on *Star Trek: The Next Generation*. On that day, Lt. Commander Jordie LaForge was in no mood for conversation. I followed his eyes to a woman standing a few feet away. I presume she was his date, and boy, did she look upset.

When Burton turned his eyes toward me, I was on the receiving end of a look angrier and more agitated than Kunta Kinti's face when he was forced to take the slave name Toby. In the blink of an eye, my mood flashed from elation and admiration to embarrassment.

I believe truly great actors can illuminate a character so brilliantly that we lose our understanding of the difference between reality and fiction. In this case, it was obvious that Burton had been possessed by an alien life form. From that encounter, I learned that—if you let them—celebrities can hold sway over you.

I had a momentary flirtation with actress Lorraine Toussaint. We attended the Agape International Spiritual Center in Santa Monica and were both enamored with the empowering messages we received from Rev. Michael B. Beckwith. Lorraine invited me to tea at a local restaurant after a Wednesday night service. I found myself drawn to her verbose, yet reassuring manner. I found her full lips sexy and the characteristic gap between her two front teeth oddly appealing. We hung together on many an evening before I discovered she was an actress. It was an aha moment when I learned she played a character (in the Bruce Willis movie *Hudson Hawk*) who brought me to tears with laughter.

I was in a committed relationship at the time. So I put the brakes on. She went on to become a Hollywood star, and I was thrilled whenever I saw her on television. She had a recurring role as defense lawyer Shambala Green on *Law and Order*. But soon she was popping up everywhere; her IMDB bio credits her with more than thirty guest appearances on television shows. She had an equally fruitful career on the big screen. She later played Boynton Robinson in the 2014 historical drama film *Selma*.

I think fondly of Lorraine and often regret that I never once tasted her now famous lips.

Once, while I was a reporter for KTLA Los Angeles, I was diverted from an assignment and told to roll to Los Angeles International Airport. In anticipation of the arrival of Air Force Two, an entire section of the airport had been closed. Some celebrity encounters shock and amaze. This was such an encounter, as then-Vice President Dan Quayle disembarked. I couldn't wait for the photographer to take some video and hand off the tape so I could take it back to the station and write a quick voiceover on the vice president's L.A. visit. As the VP disembarked, he decided to glad-hand the media. His eyes were glued to me when he walked down the steps of Air Force Two. He walked straight toward me, introduced himself, and offered his hand. What do you do when the Vice President of the United States offers you his hand? You shake it! I'll admit, I expected to get a "wet noodle," but Dan Quayle left a lasting impression with a grip that would put an NFL linebacker to shame. I immediately took notice, squeezed back, gazed into his eyes, and thought, "Wow. What a powerful handshake."

Members of the local media were mesmerized by the impromptu lovefest. They later teased that Dan Quayle had a man crush on me.

I had another opportunity to meet Dan Quayle a couple of years later at a symposium he was attending at Sacramento State University. I set aside a quiet classroom to chat with him about the symposium and why he was there. When the camera stopped rolling, our short chat evolved into a deep, extended conversation. An hour later, I was a Dan Quayle fan for life.

The Vice President even explained his infamous "potato*e*" blunder. Quayle was officiating a spelling bee at Ed Muñoz Riviera elementary school in Trenton, New Jersey in 1992 when he altered a twelve-year-old boy's correct spelling of the word *potato* to include the letter "E" at the end. Quayle insisted he knew the boy's spelling was correct, but the school cue card had the letter E at the end. He also told me spelling bee officials told him the boy's spelling was not correct.

Vice President Dan Quayle's blunders are likely too many to count. He butchered the United Negro College Fund's slogan, "A mind is a terrible thing to waste." Quayle said, "You take the UNCF model that what a waste it is to lose one's mind, or not to have a mind is being very wasteful. How true that is."

I never got over my man crush on Dan Quayle. In fact, for a minute, I considered titling this book "Dan Quayle is Really Smart."

Say what you will, but Dan Quayle is intelligent, compassionate, and, above all, optimistic. As he once stated, and I truly believe, "The future will be better tomorrow."

Finally, on celebrity encounters, while in Florida, a Hispanic man approached me with a broad smile on his face. "Paul Jackson... You're Paul Jackson. You are famous in Panama," he told me, then explained that the station I worked for in Denver (KMGH-TV) was on cable in Panama. Since most Panamanians are black, the audience apparently adored me and anchor Bertha Lynn.

At that point, it became clear to me that celebrity, much like beauty, is in the eye of the beholder.

CHAPTER 37

THE HAWK'S MESSAGE

I could almost hear the color of the sky on that fall day in Glenside, a small suburban enclave that abuts Philadelphia. The temperature dipped suddenly as the north wind made itself known, chilling the air around me. Above, the first of the wild geese were beginning their noisy winter migration. Suddenly, the trees in my neighborhood began to whisper to one another. After their short confab, the pines began to drop their needles in unison like a golden rain, giving the ground a soft pale glow. The tall oaks were also part of the wind song; with a burst, their colors seemed to change before my eyes. Their beautiful hue made me feel warm inside, even though I felt somewhat melancholy over the coming winter.

Another season had passed; another year stalled in this place called Pennsylvania. Over long periods, the suburban landscape can dull your senses and pull you into a gentle hibernation. The trappings of everyday life can draw you deeper into the coma that is suburbia.

Brilliance is lost to the monochromatic drone of the middle class, where encounters with neighbors are limited to plants and animals, and on occasion, schools or taxes.

Oddly enough, there is a peace and order here, but I was filled with a sense of futility.

On January 2, 2006, I walked outside my home and was greeted by weather that seemed almost like spring. Instantaneously, a sense of total clarity and connection with everything seen and unseen filled my being. I had an intense knowing that a long-awaited shift of consciousness had occurred deep within me some time during the night.

The day before, I was out with a sickness that had all the symptoms of food poisoning. I was dehydrated, but every attempt to drink led to heaves so violent that Amy called the hospital. After describing my condition, an on-call E.R. doctor said it was possible I'd ripped a muscle from my ribcage and should come in immediately. During the course of that New Year's Day, it felt as if my body were commanding my mind to release and let go. Instead of going to the E.R., I collapsed onto the hardwood floor in my bedroom and fell into a deep sleep.

When I awoke the next day, it felt like I'd purged the poison in my system. I felt lighter. As I walked outside for a breath of fresh air, something wonderful happened. A great hawk swooped down on me, missing my head by inches. Still dazed from my sudden illness, I had no thought of screaming. I simply turned and watched as the mighty bird made a U-turn, landed on the branch of an oak tree above me, and looked down to study me. I immediately took the opportunity to tell this magnificent bird how wonderful it was, and that its mere presence had just made my year. It seemed to reply to me telepathically. I sensed a great healing had taken place. "You can begin anew," said the voice. The hawk and I admired one another in the warm silence of the afternoon. Then, as suddenly as it appeared, this master of telekinesis lifted its wings and ascended. As it moved upward, it seemed to intensify the color of the sky. A few seconds later, it gently touched down in a higher tree about 100 feet away. It turned again, facing me. I thanked it, and then called my two daughters outside so they could see this stately creature. Only Katelyn made it outside in time to see this great messenger of hope take flight. As it disappeared into the sky, I sensed it saying, "With Spirit, anything is possible, anything. Begin anew." A sense of warmth and well-being washed over me.

As Kyra Skye rushed outside, her face wore her disappointment in missing the hawk. I smiled and told her, "Don't worry; it will be back." And then, I pointed to my heart and said, "It lives here now."

EPILOGUE

The hawk became my totem, my spirit guide. It appears to me whenever I doubt the existence of God/Source energy.

The appearance of my great hawk prompted me to begin this memoir.

By unleashing the past, I desired to obliterate stereotypes about black men in American society. Though not mentioned previously in these pages, I knew early in life that the negative perceptions about minorities, especially black men, were falsehoods perpetrated by a biased media. If there is anyone who doubts many significant achievements of African Americans have been erased from history by mainstream media, I challenge you to examine my career in broadcasting.

Who helped pioneer Southern California's first local twenty-four-hour cable news operation? How did David Gregory get his big break at NBC News? Who was among the first journalists on the airways in Los Angeles after a devastating earthquake rocked the city?

When I requested a look into the station's archives, no one at KCBS-TV could locate an air-check (recording) of me informing the Southland that, "Southern California had experienced a significant seismic event." In fact, I found my coverage was omitted. A significant piece of history was gone.

The *Los Angeles Times* praised Hal Fishman's earthquake coverage, but omitted the fact that a young African American reporter brought him up to speed on the events live on the air.

While in Sacramento at KCRA TV, I covered the hundred-year floods that devastated northern California. I unearthed shocking information that revealed local authorities were informed firsthand of failing levees along the Sacramento River, but failed to act on the information. This led to at least one fatality. The information I compiled while covering this event was the meat of a flood special presented by the station. My reports were taken word for word and rebroadcast. Yet no one ever bothered to follow up on the events I'd reported a week earlier. Everyone involved with that special, except me, received the prestigious Northern California Emmy.

Original reports have been erased from the official record by the media, who are the record keepers.

In large part, today's television news broadcast will become tomorrow's history text. But what happens when that text is edited, or erased?

History is lost, or changed....

And so this memoir serves to fill in the gaps. It points out that all black men are not criminals. Additionally, tall black men have the capacity to be much more than basketball players. We are not always absentee fathers, either.

It was a profound journey from the twentieth century to this new age. My stories do not end here. The hawk reminds me that each of us must begin anew with every sunrise, and every waking breath. I have come to believe there is no coincidence in the universe...only synchronicity.

As a child, I came close to death, hanging alone from the rusty chains of a broken swing set in our backyard in Compton. Perhaps I was spared that day in order to relay this information to you.

But I had a knowing, an inner knowledge of something beyond. It was nearer to me than my scratched and bleeding neck and dangling feet. As I gasped for my last breath, I knew I had nothing to fear. The Presence that is life itself— The Force—was with me.... As it was in the beginning, it is now and ever shall be with me...Always.

ABOUT THE AUTHOR

 A graduate of Portland State University, and fortunate enough to be invited to try out for the Portland Trailblazers, Paul Jackson looked beyond sports. Pursuing his lifelong dream of becoming a broadcaster, he waived an opportunity to play professional basketball in Europe, and instead leveraged his B.S. in communications to secure a job in radio.

Jackson started his career as a page for popular radio station KYTE Portland, Oregon. Mentored by local legends, Jackson excelled quickly, becoming the station's Sports Director before moving onto KJR, Seattle, in the same position. Moving forward, Jackson pushed into news at KOMO, Seattle, then on to well-respected radio stations KGW, Portland, and KOA, Denver.

In 1986, Jackson made the transition to television as a sports reporter for KMGH, Denver. There he was embraced by members of the N.B.A. Nuggets, who had previously declined interviews with the media. Later, he burst on the scene in Oklahoma as Tulsa's first full-time African American sports anchor on KOTV. Again he was embraced, this time by coaching legends Barry Switzer, Billy Tubbs, and Nolan Richardson as a straight-shooting former athlete-turned-journalist.

Throughout the years, Jackson's exceptional work in broadcast journalism has been recognized with numerous awards, including two Emmys for live news coverage and the prestigious RTNDA Golden Mic. Jackson was the first reporter on the air during the 1994 Northridge earthquake.

Reporting from a badly damaged broadcast center at KCBS-TV, Jackson informed the nation that "Southern California has experienced a significant seismic event."

Jackson was one of the pioneers of the Orange County News Channel, the region's first local 24-hour cable news operation. As weekend anchor and reporter, he left his indelible imprint on OCN through hard-hitting stories, memorable features, and electrifying live shots.

He went on to become one of the most recognized freelance television journalists in Los Angeles. He was a fixture at KTLA, where his aggressive reporting style was clearly reflected in his courageous coverage of the L.A. Riots. As fate would have it, Jackson was also one of the first broadcasters on the air during the 1992 Big Bear-Landers Quakes. From the anchor desk, he reported the story until the full resources of the station could be mobilized. Jackson recalls, "The *L.A. Times* media section reported Hal Fishman's command of the airwaves that fateful day. But as I rushed off the set when the master arrived, Hal asked me to remain so that I could bring him up to speed live on the air. It was one of the most memorable days of my career."

Jackson's ability to keep KTLA ahead of the competition was rewarded with a live truck and two-man crew, dispatched to the seismology lab at Cal Tech. They arrived in time to watch the Richter scale record the magnitude 7.3 Landers Quake, part two of the now infamous twin quakes that jolted the Southland.

Also for KTLA, with cameras rolling, Jackson orchestrated a fugitive surrender, safely delivering an accused murder suspect to the LAPD. The trusted journalist also covered breaking news for KTTV and KCOP. When not on television, Jackson was in high demand as a news reporter for KFWB and KNX radio. While in his hometown of Los Angeles, Jackson did as the natives do and got a taste of Hollywood — playing himself on the big screen in the motion picture "*Jimmy Hollywood.*" But the stars were calling elsewhere.

In 1994, Jackson became a staff reporter at KCRA-TV in Sacramento. His flair for live news reporting and experience as an outdoorsman helped earn Jackson and the station several Emmys for its coverage of the 100-year flood that devastated Northern California.

Further success took Jackson to the Northeast for a stint as a general assignment news reporter at Philadelphia's NBC-10 from 1997 to 2000. Since then, he has seen action at KYW-TV, Philadelphia; WFMZ, Allentown; WWOR, New York; BET Nightly News; WDEL Wilmington, Del, New York 1 and WHYY-FM, Philadelphia.

Standing 6'10" tall, Paul Jackson has a different view. He is a self-proclaimed expert on human ergonomics and ranked the best light trucks and SUVs for XLTs (the big and tall) in the feature story "Living Large" and other articles for Motor Trend's *Truck Trend Magazine.* He has also published automotive features in *The Philadelphia Tribune* and editorial commentaries in *The Philadelphia Inquirer.*

Jackson is currently a broadcast journalist, writer and voice actor and now author.